EC TRANSPORT LAW

ROSA GREAVES

Longman

An imprint of Pearson Education

Harlow, England · London · New York · Reading, Massachusetts · San Francisco
Toronto · Don Mills, Ontario · Sydney · Tokyo · Singapore · Hong Kong · Seoul
Taipei · Cape Town · Madrid · Mexico City · Amsterdam · Munich · Paris · Milan

Pearson Education Limited

Edinburgh Gate
Harlow
Essex CM20 2JE
England

and Associated Companies throughout the world

Visit us on the World Wide Web at:
www.pearsoneduc.com

First published 2000

ISBN 0-582-41425-3

British Library Cataloguing-in-Publication Data
A catalogue record for this book is available from the British Library

Library of Congress Cataloging-in-Publication Data
A catalog record for this book is available from the Library of Congress

Set by 7 in 10/13 pt Sabon
Printed in Great Britain by Henry Ling Ltd., at the Dorset Press,
Dorchester, Dorset.

CONTENTS

SERIES PREFACE

The Longman European Law Series is the first comprehensive series of topic-based books on EC law aimed primarily at a student readership, though I have no doubt that they will also be found useful by academic colleagues and interested practitioners. It has become more and more difficult for a single course or a single book to deal comprehensively with all the major topics of Community law, and the intention of this series is to enable students and teachers to 'mix and match' topics which they find to be of interest: it may also be hoped that the publication of this Series will encourage the study of areas of Community law which have historically been neglected in degree courses. However, while the Series may have a student readership in mind, the authors have been encouraged to take an academic and critical approach, placing each topic in its overall Community context, and also in its socio-economic and political context where relevant.

The EC Treaty has always contained a Title on Transport, requiring the creation of a common transport policy, just as it has always required the development of a common agricultural policy. While transport policy has taken considerably longer to develop, it may be suggested that, for example, the opening-up of the market in air transport has been one of the Community's great achievements, particularly for those of us who are regular travellers to the rest of Europe from regional airports. However, Community transport policy is not just a matter of opening-up the market. It has an important social content, exemplified at an early stage by the drivers' hours legislation, and it has had important constitutional effects, since it is in this area that the concept of implied external competence for the Community was developed. I am most grateful to Professor Greaves, who has long taken a particular interest in EC transport policy, for presenting and analysing so clearly what is nowadays a very wide range of material.

John A. Usher

Dedicated to my mother
Teresinha da Silva Costa Greaves

AUTHOR'S PREFACE

The title 'EC Transport Law' may give the impression that this monograph covers all the legislative measures and case-law pertinent to the transport industry. However, such comprehensive work cannot be undertaken within the constraints of the word limit imposed for the Euoropean Law Series. The structure and content of the monograph reflect a personal choice to concentrate on areas less covered by the literature.

Within the general aims of this Series, the specific aim of this book is to provide a succinct and reader-friendly account of those Community legislative measures which form the core of EC Transport Law, and which have been adopted within the ambit of establishing a Common Transport Policy as required by the 1957 Treaty of Rome. Chapter 1 traces the development of the Common Transport Policy up to the 1990s, while Chapter 2 sets out the Legislative Framework.

The following chapters (Chapters 3 to 5) reflect the decision to focus on the specific measures adopted to liberalize the industry. Furthermore, after much reflection, it was decided to structure the chapters horizontally: instead of dealing with each mode of transport separately, it was decided to take up themes and apply them, as far as it is possible, across all modes of transport. Chapters 3 and 4 are concerned with positive liberalization, meaning measures adopted in order to remove obstacles to access to the internal market. The decision to use two chapters was not taken as a matter of principle but primarily to make the chapters shorter. The decision can, however, be justified since the obstacles to access for the maritime and air transport service providers are arguably less problematic as a whole (because of their international nature) than the obstacles for those providing inland mode transport services. Chapter 5 concerns indirect liberalization, meaning the harmonization of those member states' laws concerned with the operation of national markets. National laws may defeat access rights if the operation in the host member state's market is made difficult by national requirements which are different from those imposed by the home state ('dual burden').

Chapter 6 is concerned with three problems which are specific to the transport industry, namely combined transport, the provision and maintenance of infrastructure and the financing of infrastructure.

Finally, Chapter 7 selects three areas of Community law and policy which have a direct impact on transport undertakings operating within the European Community. These areas comprise the Competition Rules (Arts 81 and 82 applicable to private undertakings and the Merger Regulation), state aids (Arts 87 and 88) and External Relations. Although these matters are dealt with very briefly, there is a significant amount of literature available (both generally and specific to certain modes of transport) which will assist a reader interested in pursuing them further.

In writing this book I am particularly grateful to Professor John Usher for asking me to undertake this task; to Nicholas Goodwin for his quick and good-humoured response whenever I gave him a long list of references to find or check; to Inger Hambre for assistance with library searches; to Joao Ferreira and Alejandro Martinez-Godin from the Directorate General for Transport (European Commission) for their kindness in answering my questions; and to Francis Pritchard for reading the manuscript.

Though I received help from several sources, responsibility for any errors are to be attributed to me exclusively; neither contents nor errors are in any way attributable to the persons or organizations mentioned above.

The law is stated as at 31 March 2000.

Rosa Greaves
Allen and Overy Professor of European Law
Durham European Law Institute
University of Durham
April 2000

TABLE OF CASES

TABLE OF LEGISLATION

TABLE OF TREATIES

CHAPTER 1

Introduction

The meaning of 'Common Transport Policy'

The transport industry is a difficult one to regulate. Not only are there three main sectors, inland transport, sea and air transport, each with their own special features, but there are other general factors which make the transport industry different in economic terms from other industrial sectors. The EC Treaty recognizes these differences by referring to the 'distinctive features of transport' in Art. 71 but it does not define them.

Some of these distinctive features remain relevant while others have only an historical interest. A remaining feature is the dual character of transport. On the one hand, transport is a major industry by whatever criteria it is measured: investment, employment, etc. The capital investment is huge and a large percentage of workers are employed in this industry. On the other hand, transport is an indispensable ancillary activity to other industrial sectors and so levels of rates are crucial to the state's economy. The independent carriers, in particular, occupy a central position in the market as a whole, and this requires regulation since their actions can hinder international trade by discriminating as to charges between producers or between consumers.

Another distinctive feature is that undertakings offering transport services vary in size and in economic power. The transport industry is characterized by undertakings of very dissimilar structure which nevertheless provide interchangeable services. Transport is not like a commodity that can be stocked. Inelasticity in the supply of transport, owing to the 'perishability' of its services, makes full freedom of competition impracticable. Furthermore, transport is an industry with public service obligations, where governments often intervene not only by requiring that certain services be provided but also by controlling tariffs.

Geographical factors have also had an impact on the mode of transport each member state has developed and encouraged. For example, in smaller countries such as The Netherlands, road transport has prominence because the distances are short. In Germany and France, however, the governments have promoted the railways which are more appropriate for greater distances.

Historical factors have also contributed to the distinctive features of the transport industry. First, transport measures were used as an instrument of state economic policy. Thus the development of national transport policies evolved in very different ways, depending on geographical and economic conditions and policies of the states. In the railway sector, for example, national transport policies and general national economic policies went hand-in-hand. Public financing of the infrastructure was very common. For example, Italy invested heavily in its railways in order to encourage development of the southern region of the country. Similarly, the building of roads often depends on the state providing the funds. In some countries the creation of cheap transport regardless of viability was one of the methods used to promote the industrialization of a particular underdeveloped region. Thus a fundamental problem is that the national transport systems of the member states have been developed to serve national needs which are disparate and do not facilitate integration.

Secondly, the international nature of transport inevitably resulted in the conclusion of important international agreements to which some of the member states were parties. For example, the Rhine regime, established by the Mannheim Convention of 1868, with a Central Commission implementing its provisions, governs the most important single constituent in inland transport, namely the river Rhine. Switzerland, a non-EC country, is a party to the Convention. More generally, some member states such as The Netherlands require the preservation of the maximum freedom of international transport services in order to sustain their pre-eminence in European trade. Article 307 expressly recognizes limitations imposed on EC jurisdiction by prior international agreements.

In view of the above the founders of the European Community were well aware that the transport industry could not automatically be subject to every general rule set out in the EC Treaty. Transport is a utility historically dependent on the state. The member states pursued different transport policies and proceeded from different bases for state intervention. The compromise reached was to work towards a common policy that would enable the Community to take control from the member states. The common policy was to be established by reformulating the policies of member states to form a single Community policy, which would lead to a supranational transport policy. The policy was aimed at reducing or eliminating differences in the legal and economic systems of the member states: a process of harmonization. However, since the late 1980s, when the goal of an internal market by 1992 was agreed, it has become clear that the ultimate objective was the establishment of a single internal market in the free supply of transport services. Thus the policy is centred on the liberalization of the transport services market. This was to be achieved by the adoption of Community legislative measures rather than by the harmonization of national laws. An unresolved controversial aspect of this development is whether such a market can be achieved without the adoption of a Community external transport policy.

The development of the Common Transport Policy

Article 3(f) of the EC Treaty states expressly that one of the Community's activities is the adoption of 'a common policy in the sphere of transport'. This is hardly surprising since the establishment of a common market centred on the free movement of goods, services and persons cannot be achieved without a corresponding policy for the means of transporting these goods, services and persons. Furthermore, the goal of the EC Treaty is an all-embracing economic union. It would have been an anomaly to exclude such an important economic industry as transport. Nevertheless, the EC Treaty merely lays down some procedures and a timetable for the Common Transport Policy (CTP).

The member states, for the reasons described above, were very reluctant to progress in this area. For the first thirty years of the EC, transport policy was to a large extent under the control of individual governments. This was so in spite of the clear intention of the drafters of the EC Treaty to provide the legislative basis for a Europe-wide co-ordination. An early controversy concerned the question as to whether the Community had an obligation to create a common market for transport services or whether it was sufficient to have simply a CTP. Article 70, unlike Art. 32 (Title II) which provides for a common market in agricultural products, stresses the autonomy of the transport sector and only refers to a CTP. There are two other matters that limit the scope of the CTP. First, Art. 80(2) *prima facie* excludes air and sea transport from the ambit of the CTP by stating that '[t]he Council may, acting by a qualified majority, decide whether, to what extent and by what procedure appropriate provisions may be laid down for sea and air transport'. Secondly, the measures provided in Title V to implement the CTP are vague. The only specific measures concerned rates and tariffs, the issue of licences for carriers by road and inland waterways, and the relationship between governments and the publicly owned railways. In other fields, the general provisions of the EC Treaty apply.

Thus a separate title in the Treaty, Title V (ex Title IV), was inserted into the EC Treaty setting out the legal basis for the creation of a Common Transport Policy. The CTP is one of the three common policies (the others

3

are commercial policy and agriculture and fisheries policy) specifically mentioned in Art. 3 of the Treaty as one of the activities the Community must pursue in order to establish a 'common market and an economic and monetary union ...' as described in Art. 2. However, transport policy remained, until the mid-1980s, mainly under the control of the member states. For many years attempts by the European Commission to break the deadlock failed: Commission proposals were debated but few of any significance were adopted. It was difficult to reach agreement on a CTP, and it was only after the European Court of Justice (ECJ) condemned the inactivity of the Council of Ministers in this area[1] and the Council agreed to a programme of legislative measures[2] to achieve an internal market by the end of 1992, that a CTP began to emerge as a cornerstone of the internal market. An internal market could not be established without a CTP; a CTP, if not a fully integrated transport services market, became imperative.

The special status of sea and air transport

Sea and air transport are by their very nature international modes of transport requiring negotiation and agreement with third countries. Sea transport has a long and well-established history of world-wide regulation,[3] while air transport is governed primarily by the Chicago Convention of 1944[4] and a network of bilateral agreements between governments.

At the time of the establishment of the EC, member states were not prepared to hand over to the Community's embryonic external commercial policy control over these two very important sectors of their national economy. Thus Art. 80(2) ensured that positive action by the Council was required before anything adopted as part of the CTP would apply also to air and sea transport.

The pre-1990 period

As stated earlier, the CTP developed very slowly and until the mid-1980s the measures adopted concerned mainly inland transport. In 1961 the Schaus Memorandum[5] was the first indication of the Commission's view

---

[1] Case 13/83 *European Parliament v EC Council* [1985] ECR 1513.
[2] COM (85) 310 final.
[3] Several international conventions have been signed: e.g. UN Code of Conduct of Liner Conferences (1974); International Convention for the Safety of Life at Sea (SOLAS) (1974).
[4] Convention on International Civil Aviation, United Nations Treaty Series, vol. 15, p. 296.
[5] COM (61) 50 final.

on transport policy. This was followed by the 1962 action programme,[6] which consisted of a general programme and a timetable to coordinate the development of the CTP.

The Schaus Memorandum was aimed at a type of regime whose key characteristics were stated in the form of guiding principles. These were: equality of treatment of carriers and users; financial autonomy of undertakings in transport; freedom of action by carriers; freedom of choice by transport users; and coordination of investment. The action programme identified three groups of measures. First, measures seeking to implement Art. 71(1)(a) and (b) and securing access to the market; secondly, measures establishing a common regime for fixing carriers' charges and applying the EC competition rules (Arts 81 and 82) to the transport industry; thirdly, measures to equalize the effect on transport of state intervention. Unfortunately, the Council was unable to agree on a general programme and requested the Commission to propose specific measures. Thus in 1963 the first proposal, a regulation applying the competition rules to the (inland) transport industry, was published and adopted in 1968, but only after a long debate.[7]

As far as specific measures were concerned, those adopted during this period tended to be mainly in the nature of consultation procedures. Thus in 1962 the Council adopted a Decision[8] setting out a consultation procedure requiring member states to notify the Commission and inform the other member states in good time, in writing, of all projected measures related to inland transport. Council Decision 66/161 was also adopted, setting out a consultative procedure for transport infrastructure investments.[9] The aim of this measure was to encourage a more harmonious development of transport routes within the Community, avoiding situations whereby roads leading to national borders are continued on the other side of the border by secondary roads of limited capacity.

Council Decision 65/271[10] was then adopted, laying down a programme of harmonization of certain provisions characterized as having an effect on competition in the inland sector. The Decision laid down guidelines for the harmonization of national provisions in the fields of taxation, public service obligations and social policy. These guidelines concerned not only distortions between different modes of transport but also those within the

---

[6] COM (62) 88 final.
[7] Regulation 1017/68, OJ 1968 L 175/1.
[8] JO 1962 p. 270, amended by Council Decision 73/402, OJ 1973 L 347/48.
[9] JO 1966 p. 583.
[10] JO 1965 No. 88, p. 1500.

same mode of transport and between the transport undertakings of the member states.

The programme laid down by the Decision was not completed so, after a further Commission Memorandum[11] and a memorandum submitted by the Italian delegation, Council Decision 67/790[12] was adopted to agree priorities. This Decision is regarded as one of the watersheds in the development of the CTP. Priority was given to road transport, with the establishment of a Community quota and a system of bracket tariffs for road haulage.

Thus by the end of the 1960s the Community had achieved the following: established procedures for prior consultation; implemented provisions of the EC Treaty banning discrimination and introducing a number of minor measures to facilitate transport operations within the Community; abandoned the early ambitious Action Programme; embarked on a comprehensive series of measures designed gradually to reform the structure of inland transport in the Communities; and already implemented or agreed the initial steps for the harmonization of conditions of competition. After ten years of inactivity a major shift in emphasis had taken place, from complete reliance on rate controls to a mixed programme of capacity controls and competition policies.

The accession, in 1973, of the UK, Ireland and Denmark, marked another opportunity to focus on transport. The Commission issued a Communication on the development of a transport policy[13] redefining the objectives and proposing a short-term programme for 1974–76 and a ten-year long-term programme. The aim was to open up the market, letting market forces regulate the industry, and to emphasize the role of the CTP in relation to other Community policies. It was intended that freedom of supply of transport services should emerge, users should be guaranteed a choice of services, and transport policy should be coordinated with regional policy. This policy included harmonization of competition conditions within each mode of inland transport and between modes. In addition, the Commission, for the first time, attempted a detailed analysis of the role of the state in the transport industry. It proposed adequate payment by all users of infrastructure applied by the member states. This was a change of direction, since the Commission no longer proposed to eliminate state intervention but to align intervention at Community level and use it where it met the needs of the Community as a whole.

---

[11] 10 EEC Bull. Suppl. No. 3/67.
[12] JO 1967 No. 322 p. 4.
[13] 1973 EEC Bull. Suppl. No. 16/73.

A further work programme to cover the years up to 1980 was proposed by the Commission in 1977. Although a Council decision was not adopted, the Council noted its willingness to follow the proposed list of priorities. The next work programme for the years 1981–83, drawn-up at the request of the European Parliament, was adopted by a Council Resolution which laid down ten new principles. These principles included, *inter alia*, measures for improving the situations of railways, facilitating frontier crossings and improving the efficiency and safety of transport. In 1983 the Commission, again at the request of the European Parliament, revised the work programme for the three modes of inland transport in a Communication entitled *Progress Towards a CTP – inland transport.*[14] The objectives of the 1961 Memorandum and the 1973 Communication were reiterated, namely that it is crucial for the establishment and development of the internal market to have an efficient transport system. The 1983 Communication was however much more pragmatic in its approach than the previous two documents: account was taken of the reasons for the failure of the Council to act on previous proposals.

As far as the individual modes of inland transport are concerned Community policy was very limited during this period. The 1983 Communication sought the ultimate elimination of capacity controls for road transport. Many restrictions have traditionally been imposed by member states upon road hauliers from other member states wishing to enter their territory. Although Scandinavia, the Benelux countries, Greece, Portugal, Ireland and most of Eastern Europe had free access, France, Germany, Italy and Spain limited the road transportation of goods by foreign hauliers through quotas or permits. In addition, road haulage rates for international transport were fixed by agreement between the member states concerned.

As for rail transport, the emphasis was placed on improving the efficiency and attractiveness of the services. In the nineteenth century there was much conflict between railways on the one hand, and inland waterways and coastal shipping on the other. The latter had until then enjoyed a monopoly of long-distance transportation of goods. The next challenge was during the 1920s with the appearance of road haulage. Many attempts were made to hinder the development of road haulage and protect the railways, the reason being obvious when it is considered that railways in most countries were owned by governments and operated under certain public service obligations. Further, the development of road transport was viewed

---

14 COM (83) 58 final.

negatively by most governments, since it increased public expenditure, as, for example, in the maintenance of roads and bridges, and by the population, who feared accidents and damage to buildings.

Until the 1980s Community policy on railway transport was limited to the elimination of distortion of competition and better financial transparency. Thus the development of rail routes and capacity was carried out according to national considerations and objectives, and no account was taken of traffic flows within the Community, such as the hold-up of traffic flows on the north-south routes caused by the inability of the Italian railway network to cope with the traffic.

The first time the Community showed interest in this mode of transport was in 1973, when railway transport policy was adopted providing for biennial reports from the member states on the economic and financial situation. The 1983–85 report indicated considerable risks facing railways with the liberalization of other modes of transport and this spurred the Commission into action. Before that, Community action centred on cooperation between railway undertakings[15] and on increasing the commercial independence of national railway undertakings.[16]

In the early 1980s the measures adopted were mainly concerned with the need to strengthen the cooperation between national railway systems. The Commission Memorandum of 1980 and its Action Plan of 1982 outlined the broad lines of Community policy in the railway sector. Council Resolution 82/622[17] set out these broad lines of railway policy within the framework of the CTP. It focused attention on cooperation between railway undertakings where international traffic was concerned. Attention was to be directed, *inter alia*, to: closer international cooperation; the organization of relations between railway undertakings and governments so as to give undertakings sufficient independence as regards their commercial management, and in order to enable them to adapt to market requirements and technical developments; and facilitation of and speeding up at frontier crossings.

Other measures were also adopted, such as Council Decision 83/418[18] on the commercial independence of railway undertakings in the management of their international passenger and luggage traffic, as well as Council Recommendation 84/646[19] on strengthening the cooperation of the

---

[15] e.g. Council Resolution 71/119, OJ 1971 C 5/1.
[16] e.g. Council Decision 75/327, OJ 1975 L 152/3.
[17] OJ 1982 C 157/1.
[18] OJ 1983 L 237/32.
[19] OJ 1984 L 333/63.

national railway undertakings of the member states in international passenger and goods transportation.

In 1983 the Commission set itself the objective of contributing to the creation of an environment which would reduce financial costs for railways and, at the end of 1989, the Commission submitted to the Council its proposals for an EC railways strategy, including an overall Community plan for the high-speed train (TGV). The central idea was to separate operational and infrastructure activities, enabling private trains to use public tracks. Lines and railway stations would be owned and run by a national 'railway authority'. Locomotives and wagons would be privately owned. Thus the link between the owner of the capital infrastructure and the provider of the service would come to an end. The railway networks would be operated in a similar manner to airports. The clear distinction between the ownership of infrastructure and the commercial activities to provide services would prevent cross-subsidization and distinguish between regulated and free market activities.

As to the establishment of a TGV network, there was strong support from the Commission, which cleared in July 1990, as compatible with the Treaty, a French state aid package aimed at funding the design of the future TGV. The eventual extension of the TGV network to east Europe is also being studied. In 1990 the Commission submitted plans for the liberalization of the rail freight and passenger market.

As regards inland waterways, a few measures for access to the market were proposed but these measures did not concern directly the right of market entry. Most of the inland waterway traffic of the Community is carried on the Rhine. Thus the main provisions governing the inland navigation sector are those relating to the Revised Convention for the Navigation of the Rhine (Mannheim Convention) and the 1979 Additional Protocol 2, which amended the Convention. In order to incorporate these provisions into Community law, the Council adopted Regulation 2919/85,[20] laying down the conditions for access to the arrangements under the Revised Convention relating to vessels belonging to the Rhine Navigation.

As far as maritime and air sectors are concerned, significant legislative activity started only in the mid-1980s when the first maritime package was adopted in 1986 after the publication of a Commission Memorandum.[21] The Memorandum, entitled *Progress Towards a Common Transport*

---

[20] OJ 1985 L 280/4.
[21] OJ 1985 C 212.

Policy (maritime transport), set out the main line of action for Community policy. Before 1986, maritime initiatives were based to a large extent on the 1973 Communication defining transport policy and on a 1976 Commission Communication[22] which brought about a discussion within the EC on the scope and likely content of a maritime transport policy. From 1977 onwards, several Council measures were adopted concerning three broad areas: first, consultation and collection of information in respect of the activities of third countries in the field of cargo shipping;[23] secondly, encouragement to member states to accede to international conventions;[24] and thirdly, safety and the prevention of pollution.[25]

Since the late 1970s, the Community fleet has been in a serious crisis. The size of the EC-registered fleet in world-wide shipping has decreased drastically. Over-capacity in the world market has worsened the conditions of competition of the EC shipping lines as compared with those from non-Community countries with lower costs. In addition, protectionist policies of certain non-Community countries and the unfair practices (e.g. tariff dumping) by a number of shipping lines have made the situation worse.

Some measures were taken in the late 1970s concerning air transport. After the ECJ's 1974 ruling that the general rules of the EC Treaty applied to these modes of transport,[26] the Council adopted a priority programme of measures. The programme was concerned with noise emissions from subsonic aircraft,[27] mutual recognition of qualifications of employees and harmonization of working conditions and accident investigations. A Commission Memorandum, entitled *Contributions by the European Communities to the Development of an Air Transport Service*,[28] was published. The Memorandum was concerned with tariffs, staff working conditions and qualifications.

---

[22] COM (76) 341 final.

[23] e.g. Council Decision 77/587, OJ 1977 L 239/23, the first decision taken under Art. 80(2), which set up a consultation procedure on relations between member states and third countries in shipping matters and on action relating to such matters in international organizations.

[24] e.g. Regulation 954/79, OJ 1979 L 121/1 on the ratification by member states of, or their accession to, the UN Convention on a Code of Conduct for Liner Conferences.

[25] e.g. Directive 79/116, OJ 1979 L 33/33 (subsequently amended) concerning minimum requirements for certain tankers entering or leaving Community ports.

[26] See Chapter 2 for further details.

[27] Directive 80/51, OJ 1980 L 18/26, subsequently amended.

[28] COM (79) 311.

In 1978 the Council adopted the first programme of priorities for air transport followed in 1979 by the Commission's Memorandum on the future path to be taken by air transport services.[29] The Memorandum stressed that a European regional framework for air transport had to be agreed. In 1979 a Council Decision 80/50[30] was adopted, establishing a consultation procedure for air transport links between member states and third countries and defined the action to be taken concerning the mode of transport in international agreements. In 1983 Directive 83/416[31] was adopted, seeking to replace bilateral agreements between member states by direct action from the airlines. Another Commission Memorandum[32] was published in 1984, developing the ideas expressed in the 1979 Memorandum and basing Community action on evolution rather than on revolution. The Memorandum accepted that the structure of bilateral agreements and collaboration of national airlines had to continue. The 1984 Memorandum was the basis for the first air transport package eventually adopted in 1987. This was followed by the second and third civil aviation packages of 1990 and 1992.

In evaluating this period it is clear that the Commission, as the proposer of legislative measures, started in 1973 to be much more pragmatic in its approach to formulating the CTP. The Commission identified actual problems and recognized that the economic, political and legal conditions of the transport industry differed substantially from member state to member state. Its initial difficulty was in deciding which approach to follow. Should the Commission seek to propose to the Council measures to establish the freedom to provide transport services or measures to harmonize the conditions of competition for the industry? Even though a change of emphasis took place in 1973, only in 1979 did a truly realistic approach become apparent when a decision was taken on the criteria for and the procedures in respect of the adjustment of bilateral quotas. Nevertheless, positive action only emerged after a ruling from the ECJ and the adoption of the 1985 White Paper on completing the internal market.

---

[29] 1979 EC Bull. Suppl. 5 – Contribution of the EC to the Development of Air Transport Services.

[30] OJ 1980 L 218/24.

[31] OJ 1983 L 237/19, subsequently amended.

[32] COM (84) 72 final entitled 'Progress Towards the Development of a Community Air Transport Policy'.

The ruling in *European Parliament* v *EC Council*

In the early 1980s the European Parliament took the initiative and started Art. 232 proceedings before the ECJ seeking declarations that the Council of Ministers (the decision-making body in the EC) had failed to act in the field of transport policy in breach of its Treaty obligations under Arts 3(f), 51, 70, 71 and 80 by failing to establish a CTP within the specified time-table (Art. 71(2)). In addition, the European Parliament alleged that the Council had violated the EC Treaty by neglecting to decide on Commission proposals concerned with transport (eight regulations and five directives).

The ECJ ruled that 'the absence of a common policy which the Treaty requires to be brought into being does not in itself necessarily constitute a failure to act sufficiently specific in nature to form the subject of an action under Article 175 [now Article 232]' (para. 53 of the judgment). The Court found that, despite the existence of the timetable under Art. 71(2), there was a margin of discretion left to the Council and so the failure to adopt a CTP as such was not actionable. However, the ECJ did agree that there was sufficient precision in the requirement under Art. 71(1)(a) and (b) for the enactment of rules relating to the conditions under which non-resident carriers might operate transport services within a member state. The Court ruled that although Art. 71 itself does not define the objectives and content of the rules to be adopted, the Article should be read in conjunction with the general provisions on services (Arts 49 and 50). The link between the transport provisions and those on services is to be found in Art. 51, which expressly states that the freedom to provide transport services is to be governed by Title V. The Court's jurisprudence on the general freedom to provide services was clear and sufficiently precise. This jurisprudence requires the elimination of all discrimination against a provider of services by reason of nationality or by reason of the fact that it is established in a member state other than the one in which the service is to be rendered. [33]

The Court was thus able to declare that 'in breach of the Treaty the Council has failed to ensure freedom to provide services in the sphere of international transport and to lay down the conditions under which non-resident carriers may operate transport services in member-states' (para. 70 of the judgment). However, the Court confirmed that it is for the Council alone to decide what measures to introduce for the required liberalization and to decide on priorities. This ruling therefore gave a gentle warning to the Council to adopt the necessary measures to establish a CTP.

---

[33] Case 279/80 *Webb* [1981] ECR 3305.

The Commission's 1985 White Paper

The debate on whether the EC Treaty required a CTP as opposed to a common market for transport services was ended when the Council adopted the Commission's 1985 White Paper on completing the Single European Market. The free supply of transport services throughout the Single European Market was a constituent part of the programme. The White Paper specified a list of measures which needed to be adopted in the transport field in order to complete the internal market. These included the phasing-out of quotas, the freedom to provide transport passenger services and the opening up of the air and maritime transport services market (para. 109). Furthermore, the White Paper made it clear that these measures were only part of the CTP. The CTP as a whole required the adoption of measures not directly relevant to the internal market, such as improvement of railway financing and infrastructure planning and investment (para. 112). There is no doubt that the phenomenon of 1992 affected the progress towards a CTP. The White Paper made it clear that national protectionist rules, such as the prohibition of non-resident carriers operating transport services in another member state, had to be removed, as they obstructed the completion of the internal market. International frontiers, although popular with member states as safety check points, must also disappear. In the White Paper the Commission proposed a number of measures to ensure that the right to provide transport services throughout the Community would be achieved.

In its Twentieth General Report for the year 1986, the Commission stressed its major objective as being the implementation of the principle of freedom to provide transport services and eliminating all distortions to competition by making appropriate proposals to the Council. By the end of 1986 a series of legislative measures affecting the maritime sector were adopted by the Council. One year later a package of measures concerning civil aviation were similarly adopted. In 1990 an Action Programme in the field of transport infrastructure was adopted with a view to the completion of the integrated transport market by 1992.[34] A full legislative programme concerning all modes of transport has been adopted to secure the freedom to offer transport services as well as to ensure a level playing field exists in the transport market. This latter goal has resulted in a large number of measures being adopted to harmonize technical barriers, ensure safety and protection of the environment, monitoring and reducing state intervention,

---

[34] Regulation 3359/90, OJ 1990 L 236/1.

as well as providing other alternatives to finance and maintain the necessary infrastructure.

Post-1990 period

The 1990s were a period of rapid change for the transport industry. Political, economic and technical factors came together to create a new operating environment. For example, the construction of the Channel Tunnel and the development of the high-speed rail network provided challenges for the transport industry. These changes also had an impact on the working environment.

In 1990 a number of high-level independent experts were brought together by the Commission under the name of 'Transport in the Year 2000'. Their terms of reference were to examine and advise on all the internal and external, medium- and long-term problems that would face the transport industry in the Community. The long-term goal was to draw up an overall framework for the transport market, based on the need to protect the environment and to adapt to new technologies. However, as some matters are agreed, new challenges emerge. Road transport operators wish to offer services throughout the Community unhindered, but at the same time a system has to be found, and agreed by the member states, on how to provide the necessary infrastructure and how to recover from the users the cost of repairing the damage done to the roads. Greater integration also has implications for external relations. As the Community looks towards Eastern Europe with the intention of assisting in the opening-up of new markets, common action is required in providing efficient transport infrastructure. Finally, the unprecedented development in technology has had and continues to have an important impact on the transport industry. The aim of the CTP is not only to liberalize the industry from national regulation but also to ensure that the rules are observed. It is necessary to maintain a fair, efficient, safe and environmentally conscious transport system in which different modes of transport can be seen as complementary to one another.

As stated above, 1992 marked a significant turning point in the evolution of the CTP. A comprehensive transport policy, ensuring the proper functioning of the Community's transport systems rather than simply the elimination of regulatory barriers to the provision of transport services, was the new objective. This new approach of 'sustainable mobility for the Community as a whole' was signalled in the 1992 Commission Communication entitled *The Future Development of the Community's Transport Policy.*[35] The Communication sets out in Annex III the follow-

---

[35] COM (92) 494 final.

ing priorities: development and integration of Community transport systems (economic and regulatory framework; technical harmonization; research and development; and network development); safety; environment protection; social protection; and external relations. The Communication stated that this approach is based on seven pillars (para. 40). First, an internal market which works efficiently and facilitates the free movement of goods and people. Secondly, a coherent integrated transport system using the most appropriate technologies. Thirdly, a trans-European transport network which interconnects national networks, makes them interoperable and links the peripheral regions of the Union with the centre. Fourthly, respect for the environment embodied in transport systems which help resolve major environmental problems. Fifthly, promotion of the highest possible safety standards. Sixthly, social policies to protect and promote the interests of those working in and using transport. Seventhly, developing relations with non-Community countries.

The priorities that emerged from the Maastricht Treaty on European Union (TEU) not only focused on the further development of the single market but also underlined the importance of other objectives. The key objective of the CTP is to ensure that transport infrastructures and transport services help business to trade and to facilitate the movement of goods and people safely throughout and beyond the Community. The measures planned to achieve the above objective were set out by the Commission in 1995.[36] The programme has three main objectives: first, to improve the quality of transport systems in terms of competitiveness, safety and environmental impact; secondly, to improve the functioning of the Single Market to promote efficiency and choice; thirdly, to broaden the external dimension by improving links with third countries.

In 1998 the Commission updated the 1995 Action Programme in a Communication entitled *Sustainable Mobility: Perspectives for the Future*, where it defined the major priorities for a CTP up to 2004 and listed the initiatives to be taken.[37]

Concluding observations

After a very slow start, considerable progress was made during the 1990s in the adoption of measures within the framework of a CTP. The areas where progress has been slower are concerned with the financing and maintenance of infrastructure and external relations.

---

[36] COM (95) 302, the CTP Action Programme 1995–2000.
[37] COM (98) 716.

CHAPTER 2

The legislative framework

The legal basis of the CTP

The EC Treaty is written like a code of law. It lays down basic principles and objectives and grants powers to the Council and the Commission to enact measures in order to achieve these objectives. Some policies need more implementing measures than others. Unable to agree on the contents of a CTP, the drafters of the Treaty bequeathed the task of formulating the policy to the Council, instructing it under Art. 71(1) to take account of the distinctive features of transport, as described in Chapter 1. Thus much was left to be discussed and agreed after the Community had been established.

Application of general EC Treaty rules

A crucial issue concerned the question as to whether Title V (Arts 70 to 80 (the transport provisions)) represented the final rules on the transport industry. Did these provisions exclude the application of other parts of the Treaty to transport, such as, for example, the Treaty provision on the free movement of persons (Arts 39 to 55)? The alternative argument was that the general rules of the Treaty applied to transport in the same way that they applied to other economic fields, and that Arts 70 to 80 were merely modifications of the general rules. This debate turned on the underlying economic and political contradictions, and particularly on the meaning of the expression 'taking into account the distinctive features of transport' found in Art. 71.

The issue was settled in *Commission v France*[1] which concerned the rights of nationals from another member state to seek employment on French ships. Under French law a proportion of the crew on a French ship (as laid down by order of the appropriate Minister) must be of French nationality. The Commission brought Art. 226 proceedings against France.

---

[1] Case 167/73 [1974] ECR 359.

The ECJ declared, agreeing with the Commission, that the general rules of the Treaty applied in the field of transport (including air and sea), except where transport was expressly excluded by the Treaty. For example, the Treaty rules concerning the freedom to provide services (Arts 49 to 55) are not applicable to the transport industry. Article 51(1) specifically states that services in the transport industry are governed by the treaty rules on transport (Title V). This ruling of the ECJ was particularly important in view of the fact that a CTP was significantly delayed.

Another set of EC Treaty provisions relevant to the transport industry are the free movement of goods rules (Arts 28 to 30). For example, the ECJ has ruled[2] that national measures which did not permit the testing, for registration purposes, of buses more than seven years old imported from another member state, were an obstacle to intra-Community trade and therefore contrary to Art. 28 EC: the national measures did not apply to buses previously used in the national territory. However, the wide interpretation given to the phrase 'measures having equivalent effect' to quantitative restriction in Art. 28 does not apply to matters which are the proper subject of the CTP such as minimum freight rates.[3]

Other relevant Treaty provisions such as the EC competition rules (Arts 81 to 86), state aids (Arts 87 to 89) and taxation, were not rigorously applied to this industry until the late 1980s, when specific legislative measures affecting the transport industry were enacted.

The EC Treaty transport provisions

As stated in Chapter 1, at the time the EC Treaty was concluded, it would have been very difficult to subject the transport industry to the general rules of the Treaty without qualification. Member states had too many vested interests to protect and the conditions under which the industry operated varied greatly from member state to member state. Agreement at the 1955 Massina Conference was therefore only reached on very vague principles to guide the member states as to future action in implementing a CTP. There was no doubt that transport was an important element in establishing a Common Market but, like agriculture, the policy to be agreed and the legislative measures necessary to implement that policy had to be a matter of negotiation and compromise. Although the need for a transport network was recognized, no provisions on coordination of trans-

---

[2] Case 50/83 *Commission v Italy* [1984] ECR 1633.
[3] See judgment of the German Federal Supreme Court in Case II ZR 202/80 *Re Inland Shipping Rental Charges* [1982] 2 CMLR 808.

port were incorporated in the EC Treaty. A separate Title where the agreed vague principles, primarily concerned with the removal of discrimination, were set out was the only realistic option. The brief survey of these provisions that follows illustrates the point clearly.

Article 70

This short provision simply states that the objectives of the EC Treaty in the sphere of transport are to be achieved within the framework of a CTP as required by Art. 3(f). As already discussed, apart from this requirement of coherence in action and cooperation on the part of the member states, nothing more can be concluded from the provision as to what is meant by CTP. The wording of the Article has also been relied in argument to show that it is the Community, rather than each individual member state, that has a mandate to act in transport matters, including perhaps the conclusion of international agreements.

Article 71

This is one of the most important provisions providing the legal basis for action. Measures necessary to achieve the CTP are to be adopted by the Council, acting in accordance with the procedure set out in Art. 251 (co-decision with the European Parliament). However the goals of the policy are not specified.

Article 71 has its own limitations. Article 71(1)(a) requires the Council to adopt common measures applicable to transport between or across member states or between member states and a third country. Since it is often difficult to distinguish clearly between national and international transport, specific measures have had to be based not only on Art. 71(1)(a) but also on Art. 71(1)(d). This latter provision contains the residual power to enact 'any other appropriate provisions' for the implementation of Art. 70. Thus this legal base has been used for measures dealing with transport entirely within one member state or in the enactment of specific rules, for example in the competition field.[4] The ECJ in *Commission v Council* (the *ERTA* case)[5] stated that Art. 71(1)(d) could be used as the legal basis for the conclusion of agreements between the Community and third countries even where a specific Treaty provision, giving the Community treaty-making powers in the area concerned, was lacking.

Article 71(1)(b) lays down the conditions under which non-resident car-

---

[4] Regulation 1017/68 OJ 1968 L 175/1, applying the EC competition rules to inland transport.

[5] Case 22/70 [1971] ECR 263.

riers may operate within the member states. The Article appears to apply only to common carriers and not to own-account carriers.

A subsequent amendment to Art. 71, introduced by the Treaty on European Union, is Art. 71(1)(c) requiring the adoption of 'measures to improve transport safety'. This obligation reflects concerns that have emerged since the adoption of the original EC Treaty in the 1950s. There have also been deletions. For example, the original Article required the implementation of these obligations by the end of the transitional period which expired at the end of 1969. This provision provided the legal basis for the action taken against the Council by the European Parliament in the mid-1980s[6] discussed in Chapter 1.

A safeguard provision is included in Art. 71. Subsection 2 protects the interests of the member states by requiring unanimity from the Council where the measures may have a serious impact on the standard of living or on employment in certain areas or on the operation of transport facilities. The Council is also required to take into account the necessity to adapt to the economic developments caused by the establishment of the Common Market. These interests, namely equal treatment, financial independence and economic viability of transport undertakings, freedom of choice as to the means of transport and coordination of investment by public authorities, were reflected in the 1961 Commission Memorandum and in the 1973 Commission Communication.

It is clear from the wording of Art. 71 that there was not much consensus amongst the original member states as to what measures a CTP would entail. It could even be implied that there was little enthusiasm for action. Article 74, described below, offers further support for this conclusion. A glaring omission in Art. 71 is the lack of provision of infrastructure for the industry.

Article 72

This Article lays down a standstill rule preventing the introduction of or an increase in existing discriminatory measures between nationals of member states without unanimous approval of the Council. The Article does not prohibit discrimination as such, only any increase in discriminatory practices. Another Article aimed against discrimination is Art. 76, discussed below. Council Decision of 21 March 1962[7] requires member states to notify the Commission of measures that are likely to interfere in substance with the achievement of the CTP.

---

[6] Case 13/83 [1985] ECR 1513.
[7] JO 1962 p. 720.

Article 73

This article complements the general state aids provisions, namely Arts 87 to 89 of the EC Treaty. State aids refer to subsidies and other measures which public authorities give to industrial and commercial undertakings, and are generally considered to distort competition. This Article exempts defined categories of state aid relating to transport from the general prohibition. There are two further exemptions. The first is where the aid meets 'the needs of coordination of transport'. This type of aid has never been precisely defined. The second is where the aid is a 'reimbursement for the discharge of certain obligations inherent in the concept of a public service'. This refers mainly to the well-defined and established practices relating to a process whereby the state compensates undertakings for the cost of providing services which the undertakings are required to provide by law or acts of a public authority. Public service obligations, a concept which originates from French administrative law, have been defined in Art. 2 of Regulation 1191/69[8] and clarified by the ECJ in *Netherlands Railway Company of Utrecht v Netherlands Minister of Transport and Waterways*.[9]

Article 74

This Article qualifies the method and the extent to which a public authority may intervene in the commercial activities of carriers. The provision requires account to be taken of the 'economic circumstances of carriers' where measures are taken in respect of transport rates and conditions. This great concern for the viability of a particular participant in the transport process has no parallel in the EC Treaty except in the agriculture industry. It is also likely that the provision applies only to goods and not to passengers.

Article 75

This Article provides that discrimination in rates and conditions for transporting goods (not passengers) is to be eliminated. It imposed a duty on the Council which was discharged with the adoption of Regulation No. 11.[10] The Article applies to all carriers engaged in the transport of goods, including government-operated railways. It also applies to undertakings that set their own rates and are not subject to government controls.

---

[8] OJ 1969 L 156/1.
[9] Case 36/73 [1973] ECR 1299.
[10] JO 1960 p. 1121.

The type of discrimination referred to consists in applying different conditions to the transport of the same goods over the same routes, where the different conditions are based on the country of origin or destination of the goods and not on other justifiable considerations. This means that the transport of goods intended for another member state must be subject to the same rates as domestic traffic.

This Article complements Arts 23 to 31 of the EC Treaty, which set out the rules governing the free movement of goods.

Article 76

This Article prohibits specially favourable transport rates and conditions regulated by state authorities for the benefit of particular undertakings, in order to discriminate against other undertakings. Thus the fundamental general principle of non-discrimination on the grounds of nationality enshrined in Art. 12 of the Treaty is expressly applied to the transport industry.

The prohibition applies only to transport services carried out within the Community, rates and conditions imposed by member states, and rates and conditions created for the benefit of one or more undertakings or industries. Article 75, being directed at the member states themselves, complements Arts 87 to 89 on state aids. However, as under the state aid provisions, the Commission may authorize such support rates or conditions if it reaches a conclusion that this would be appropriate in the circumstances.

A member state wishing to introduce a special rate must first request authorization from the Commission. The Commission must then consult all the member states and, when exercising its discretion on whether to grant authorization, has to take certain special aspects of the situation into account. These are: the requirements of regional policy; the needs of underdeveloped areas and the problems of areas seriously affected by political circumstances; and the effect of the rates and conditions on competition between different forms of transport. The first two aspects are to be balanced against the last. The Commission has reviewed all the published tariffs for the three modes of inland transport. Some have been eliminated, whereas others have been modified. Very few have been approved.

Article 77

This Article requires charges levied at frontier crossings to be related to actual costs. The provision supplements Art. 25 of the Treaty (elimination of custom duties by reason of crossing a frontier).

Article 78

This Article specifically permits state aid in transport in respect of areas of Germany in order to compensate for the economic disadvantages caused by the division of Germany. There is no need to seek approval from the Commission or from the Council for such aid which would otherwise be incompatible with the CTP.

Article 79

This Article sets up an Advisory Committee for consultation by the Commission. The Committee is not involved in drafting the proposals. Its function is purely to advise on specific problems of transport policy of a legal, technical or constitutional nature. The Committee is composed of national experts. The rules of the Committee are to be found in Council Decision of 15 September 1958.[11]

Each member state proposes one or two experts, usually senior officials from the national transport ministries. In addition, member states may designate a maximum of three people who have particular expertise in each of the road, rail and inland waterway modes of transport. The experts are appointed in their personal capacity and must not be subject to national mandates. The Committee elects its chairman by absolute majority of those members present and voting. The Committee is convened by its chair at the request of the Commission. The opinions expressed by the members are presented to the Commission in the form of a report. This Committee has not played a very significant role in the development of the CTP. Undoubtedly, it duplicates the work of the Council's own working groups on transport, which examine the Commission's proposals.

Article 80

Article 80 expressly states that Arts 74 to 83 apply to inland transport only. However, para. 2 provides that the Council may, following a specified procedure, extend the provisions on inland transport to sea and air sectors. Nevertheless, as discussed above, this Article does not prevent the application of the general rules of the EC Treaty to sea and air transport.

Secondary legislation

The scheme of the EC Treaty is that where only general principles are laid down, as in Title V, the obligation to implement the principles is discharged by the adoption of EC measures. Some of these measures are

---

[11] JO 1958 p. 509.

binding, others are more akin to guidelines. There are three types of legally binding measure, namely regulations, directives and decisions set out in Art. 249. Recommendations and opinions are also mentioned in the Article but they are expressly stated to have no binding effect.

Regulations are binding and directly applicable in all the member states. Normally, as soon as the regulation is published it becomes part of the national legal order and can be pleaded before national courts as if it had been adopted by the national legislature. An example of such a regulation is Regulation 141/62,[12] which suspended the application of Regulation 17,[13] implementing the competition rules to the transport industry.

Directives are addressed to one or all the member states, requiring the addressee, within the specified period stated in the directive itself, to take the necessary steps within the national legal order to ensure that the objectives of the directive are achieved. Thus, directives give the member states the freedom to choose the most suitable form or method to achieve the end result, taking into account national characteristics.

Decisions are also binding in their entirety, but only upon those to whom they are addressed: this may be a member state, an individual or an undertaking.

The legislator

The Council is the primary legislative body in the Community's decision-making process but the Commission and the European Parliament may also exercise legislative competence.

The Commission may have competence directly conferred by the EC Treaty or under delegation from the Council. Commission legislative measures are rare in the field of transport and where they occur is because of delegation from the Council. In some areas, such as the harmonization of technical standards and social legislation, the practice has been for the Council to adopt the basic directive laying down the agreed rules and conferring competence on the Commission to adapt each directive to technical progress as and when required. The Council sometimes also adopts a framework directive, whereby the Commission is then required to adopt detailed legislation implementing the directive. This is particularly common in technical areas requiring negotiation and agreement with several interested parties and where the resulting legislative act will be very detailed. In both cases the Commission is assisted in the formulation and

[12] JO 1962 p. 2751.
[13] OJ Sp. Ed. 1962, No. 204/62, p. 87.

implementation of Community policy by Joint Committees set up for each mode of transport.

The co-decision procedure

Unlike the Commission, the European Parliament has no competence to adopt legislation on its own. However, the Treaty of Maastricht granted the European Parliament a significant role in the Community's legislative process by introducing a co-decision procedure (European Parliament and the Council) for the adoption of Community measures wherever specified in the EC Treaty. The procedure is outlined in Art. 251. Article 71(1) requires the measures implementing Art. 70 to be adopted in accordance with that procedure. In addition, Art. 71 requires the Council to consult the Economic and Social Committee and the Committee of the Regions.

The co-decision procedure requires a proposal from the Commission followed by an opinion from the European Parliament before the Council can adopt the measure. If the Parliament proposes amendments which the Council cannot approve then the Council must adopt a Common Position. If, within three months, the Parliament accepts the Common Position or takes no decision, the measure is deemed to have been adopted. If the Parliament rejects the Common Position by an absolute majority of its component members, the measure is deemed not to have been adopted. However, if the Parliament proposes amendments to the Common Position by absolute majority of its component members, the amended text is sent to the Council and to the Commission for an opinion. If, within three months, the Council accepts, by qualified majority, the amendments made by Parliament, the measure will be deemed to have been adopted. However, where the Commission has given a negative opinion to the amendments made by Parliament, there must be unanimity in the Council before Parliament's amendments are accepted. In a situation where the Council does not accept the amendments made by Parliament, a Conciliation Committee consisting of representatives of the Council and of the Parliament will be convened, within six weeks, by the President of the Council, in agreement with the President of the Parliament. The Commission also takes part but does not vote. Another six-week period is given for agreement to be reached between the two institutions. Voting in the Conciliation Committee is by qualified majority by the Council representatives and by majority of the representatives of the European Parliament.

Where no agreement is reached in the Conciliation Committee, the measure will be deemed not to have been adopted. Where agreement is reached within the six weeks, the agreed measure is sent back to the respective institutions for consideration. The European Parliament will act by absolute majority of the votes cast and the Council by qualified majority. A further period of six weeks is given for debate and voting. The measure will be deemed not to have been adopted if the period expires without a formal adoption. The relevant time periods may be extended at the initiative of either institution but only for a month in case of the initial three months and two weeks for the other periods.

In those cases, more recent legislation is no longer 'Council Directive' or 'Council Regulation' but 'Council and European Parliament Directive' or 'Council and European Parliament Regulation'.[14]

There are, however, some special cases where different procedures apply. Measures that are likely to have a major impact on living standards, employment and the operation of transport facilities are adopted by the Council acting unanimously after consulting the European Parliament and the Economic and Social Committee. Furthermore, in the case of specific measures relating to maritime or air transport, the Council decides what procedure to apply in each individual case, acting by qualified majority.

Other relevant Community measures

There are important non-binding measures adopted by the Commission which are not mentioned in the EC Treaty.

As far as the transport industry is concerned, the most important non-binding measures are 'Communications' and 'Memoranda'. Although these measures are not binding, they are important policy documents explaining not only the problems in the industry but also providing legislative drafts to solve the problems. In the transport industry Commission Communications and Memoranda are often followed by legislative action.

Since the mid-1980s the Commission has published 'White Papers' and, more recently, 'Green Papers'. This practice was copied from the United Kingdom. 'Green Papers' are consultation papers setting out the problem the Commission is attempting to solve and proposing a number of options for consultation. The paper is published and interested parties are invited to debate the problem and submit their opinions by a certain date. Then the Commission considers the views expressed and publishes a 'White

---

[14] For the purpose of this monograph, measures will be referred to as 'Directive' or 'Regulation' unless they have been adopted by the Commission.

Paper' where it justifies its preferred option, explains its rejection of other solutions and includes a draft proposal for legislation. There is no substantial difference between a 'Communication' and a 'White Paper' and nowadays Communications are often referred to as White Papers.

The European Economic Area

The European Economic Area (EEA) is a free trade area comprising the member states of the European Community plus Norway, Iceland and Liechtenstein. These countries are parties to the 1992 EEA Agreement where the non-Community countries agreed to adopt the *acquis communautaire* in return for the right of access to the internal market. The *acquis communautaire* comprises the Community rules governing the four fundamental freedoms (free movement of goods, persons, services and capital), Community measures adopted in areas closely related to the functioning of the internal market and the relevant jurisprudence from the ECJ.

In addition these three countries have agreed to 'transform' post-1992 Community legislation in the fields covered by the EEA Agreement into EEA law and thereafter implement it into their national legal orders. This does not necessarily occur at the date of publication of the legislation in the Official Journal (OJ) since, after adoption by the Community, the measures have to be adopted by a Joint EEA Council consisting of representatives of the Community and of the three countries concerned. The delay should not be longer than six months.

Thus all intra-Community transport measures apply, or will apply eventually, to these three countries. Transport measures which affect the external relations of the Community do not fall within the EEA Agreement.

The EC/ECSC relationship

For the sake of completeness a brief reference will be made to the relevant provisions of the European Coal and Steel Community Treaty (ECSC Treaty). Article 305 safeguards the provisions of the ECSC Treaty by stating that it is not superseded or modified by the EC Treaty. It follows that measures enacted under Art. 71 of the EC Treaty must not conflict with special provisions concerning rates for coal and steel products contained in Art. 70 of the ECSC Treaty. The ECSC Treaty, however, is only concerned with the transport of coal and steel. Article 4(b) of the ECSC Treaty simply prohibits discriminatory 'transport rates'. A specific chapter, containing only one Article, Art. 70, stipulates specific rules in respect of the carriage of coal and steel. Direct rail tariffs have been established for the carriage of coal and steel.

The primary concern of the ECSC transport provisions under Art. 70, para. 1, is the elimination of discrimination on the ground of nationality in transport rates and conditions in the carriage of coal and steel by requiring transparency of charges. Thus the provisions on discrimination in Art. 75 of the EC Treaty do not apply to the transport of coal and steel.[15]

Article 70, para. 3, ensures that the Commission supervises these requirements of non-discrimination by providing that scales, rates and all other tariff rules applied to coal and steel within each member state and between member states are to be published or brought to the knowledge of the Commission. Furthermore, member states are obliged (Recommendation 1/61) to adopt measures to ensure that such transparency occurs.

Upon the accession of the United Kingdom, Denmark and Ireland the Commission adopted Decision 73/152[16] requiring the publication of schedules of transport charges for routes involving intra-Community sea links. In exceptional circumstances, special rates may be authorized as a temporary measure to overcome difficulties due to unforeseen circumstances and a procedure is provided for this.

However, the provision of the ECSC Treaty reserving national jurisdiction in the field of general transport policy (Art. 70, para. 5) has been limited in its scope by Art. 70 of the EC Treaty, which provides for a CTP.[17]

The ECSC Treaty is concerned only with one economic sector, namely coal and steel, while the EC Treaty envisages a Common Market for all sectors. As far as the ECSC is concerned, railways and inland transport for coal are of primary concern. The EC Treaty, however, has a completely different starting point from that of the ECSC. Unlike the ECSC, the EC is obliged to introduce a CTP affecting all sectors of the industry. Furthermore, the rules that govern the CTP under the EC Treaty are autonomous, so that transport rules are not subordinate to policies adopted for other sectors. Under the EC Treaty power is granted to Community institutions to enact laws binding on member states.

---

[15] Article 1 of Regulation 11, see n. 10.
[16] OJ 1973 L 172/20.
[17] Case 9/61 *Netherlands v High Authority* [1962] ECR 213; Case 28/66 *Netherlands v EC Commission* [1968] ECR 1.

CHAPTER 3

Positive liberalization: access to the market for inland modes of transport

Introduction

As far as the transport industry is concerned, access to the EC market involves primarily the removal of restrictions on providing transport services between member states, on the right of a non-resident undertaking providing transport services within a member state and on access to the occupation of transport service operator. Of course, there are other practical barriers to operating in a foreign market which are due, *inter alia*, to the disparity of technical standards and social and fiscal provisions and to lack of appropriate infrastructure. These latter aspects are discussed below in Chapters 5 and 6.

As indicated in Chapter 1, the transport industry cannot be considered as a whole. The EC Treaty itself, although imposing an obligation to adopt a CTP, expressly provides for different treatment for air and sea transport compared with inland transport. The historical and economic development of each mode of transport, in each member state, also imposes a different perspective on how to liberalize these sectors and facilitate the access of the national industries to a Community-wide market.

This chapter considers measures adopted to facilitate access to the market for inland modes of transport. Similar issues relating to maritime and air transport are considered in the following chapter.

Removal of restrictions on the international carriage of goods and passengers

As far as inland transport is concerned, the idea of controlling transport movements across borders was most evident in the road sector.[1] These movements were controlled by bilateral agreements between governments.

---

[1] See 1994 report entitled *Road Freight Transport in the Single European Market* and Council Resolution of 24 October 1994, OJ C 309/4, which welcomed the report.

Substantial progress was made in the 1990s, culminating in full liberalization of road freight transport from 1 July 1998. Emphasis was then placed on facilitating international coach and bus services. In the rail sector cross border movement was hampered not directly by government action but due to different national technical standards. Directive 91/440[2] therefore established common principles for the provision of rail services. Inland waterways were not greatly affected, but in 1995 a Commission Communication on a common policy on the organization of the inland waterway transport market was published.[3] The progressive liberalization of this mode of transport (fully from 1 January 2000) was achieved in parallel with measures to reduce over-capacity and to encourage investment in inland waterway terminals.

Quotas and authorizations

Road transport (goods)

Current status

Quotas, meaning the number of authorizations that a member state may grant to its road hauliers for international journeys, was abolished on 1 January 1993.[4] Any haulier licensed in any member state is free to participate in international haulage between any two member states and to cross any other member state in the process. The concept of a capacity-based Community quota has been replaced by a quality-based Community licence.

This was a significant step in road transport policy. Thus Community quotas, bilateral quotas and quotas for transit traffic to and from non-Community countries were abolished and replaced by the Community authorization system (Community licence). Regulation 881/92[5] introduced a single Community authorization, which is granted by national competent authorities to applicants who meet the common qualitative EC criteria for access to the occupation of road haulier operator.[6] Regulation 3916/90[7] provides for safeguard measures to be taken in the event of a crisis in the market. Directive 84/647[8] was also adopted to facilitate the use of motor vehicles hired without drivers for road haulage.

---

2 OJ 1991 L 237/25.
3 COM (95) 199.
4 Regulation 1841/88, OJ 1988 L 163/1, amending Regulation 3164/76, OJ 1976 L 357/1.
5 OJ 1992 L 95/1.
6 Directive 96/26, OJ 1996 L 124/1, as amended, codified earlier measures and sets out details of the common criteria which are centred on integrity, competence and financial solvency of the applicant. See below for further details.
7 OJ 1990 L 375/10, subsequently amended.
8 OJ 1984 L 335/72, as amended by Directive 90/398, OJ 1990 L 202/46.

Background

Initially the Council adopted Directives rather than Regulations[9] as liberalization measures. Thus the first Council Directive of 23 July 1962[10] was adopted instructing member states to liberalize certain specified categories of international transport by eliminating quota and licensing restrictions. The categories, listed in Annexes,[11] concerned, for example, the carriage of mail or works of art to exhibitions or for commercial purposes. The carriage of goods (listed in Annex I) to and from a member state or in transit across that member state was exempted from any quotas or authorization schemes. Goods listed in Annex II, such as the carriage of live animals in special motor vehicles, were to continue to be subject to authorizations but not to quotas.

A few years later Directive 65/269[12] was adopted, eliminating obstacles to international road haulage which resulted from delays in the issue of authorizations as well as standardizing certain rules concerning the grant of authorizations. Authorizations were divided into three types to cater for the different needs of the applicants. The Directive applied to all cases where a member state required an authorization to be obtained before a haulier established in another member state was permitted to carry goods by road to, from or through its territory. The Directive did not apply, however, to road transport carried out under the Community's quota system, discussed below.

The Commission's policy on quotas was to allow the bilateral quota system to continue but at the same time to establish a system of Community quotas[13] which were to be increased gradually to become the general system. The system provided a number of quotas which were increased at regular intervals to a level where the supply exceeded demand. As far as hired vehicles without drivers is concerned, a proposal for a Directive replacing the 1984 Directive is in the process of being adopted.[14]

Community authorization/licence (Regulation 881/92)

The Regulation applies to the international carriage of goods by road for

---

[9] See Chapter 2 for explanation of the legal effect and the differences between these Community measures.

[10] JO 1962, p. 2005 amended subsequently by several Council Directives.

[11] The list in the Annexes was substantially amended by subsequent Directives.

[12] JO 1965, p. 1469, subsequently amended by several Directives.

[13] Regulation 1081/68, OJ 1968 L 175/13 introduced the system experimentally. The basic regulation operating the system was Regulation 3164/76, OJ 1976 L 357/1, amended subsequently by several regulations and repealed by Regulation 881/92, OJ 1992 L 95/1.

[14] OJ 1995 C 80/9.

hire or reward for journeys carried out within the territory of the Community. The Regulation covers bilateral and cross-trade journeys. Bilateral journeys refers to those where the vehicle is loaded in the member state in which it is registered and unloaded in another member state (or *vice versa*). Cross-trade journeys refers to those where the vehicle is loaded in a member state and unloaded in another member state, neither of which is the member state where the vehicle is registered. Own account carriers, that is those carrying out transport operations for non-commercial and non-profit making purposes, are exempt from obtaining a Community authorization.

Where the carriage is from a member state to a non-Community country or *vice versa*, the Regulation only applies to the part of the journey carried out within the territory of the member state of loading and unloading after the conclusion of the necessary agreements between the Community and the country concerned (Art. 1(1) and 1(2)).

International carriage is to be carried out subject to Community authorization (Art. 3(1)). The competent authorities of member states will issue a Community authorization, for a renewable period of five years (Art. 6) to any haulier carrying goods by road for hire or reward who meets the following conditions. First, the applicant is established in a member state in accordance with the legislation of that member state. Secondly, the applicant meets the conditions for being admitted to the occupation of road haulage operator to carry out the international carriage of goods by road (Art. 3(2)). Drivers must carry a certified copy of the Community authorization when carrying out international journeys between member states.

Details as to the issue of the Community authorization and of the verification procedure for member states to ensure that the authorized haulier continues to satisfy the conditions of Art. 3, are set out in Arts 5 and 7 and in Annex I. Rejection of an application has to be reasoned (Art. 8(1)) and an appeal procedure has to be provided (Art. 9). An obligation is imposed on the member state to provide annual information to the Commission on the number of road hauliers possessing Community authorizations (Art. 10) and to give each other mutual assistance in ensuring that the application and monitoring of this Regulation is carried out (Art. 11).

Safeguard measures (Regulation 3916/90)
The objective of this Regulation is to create protection against crisis and provides measures for crisis management. The Regulation also establishes a decision-making process and provides for the collection of the necessary data. The Regulation applies to international carriage of goods between member states and also to cabotage (Art. 1).

A crisis occurs when the following factors are present. First, there is serious and potentially enduring over-capacity. Secondly, there is a serious threat to the financial stability and survival of a significant number of road haulage undertakings. Thirdly, it is clear that no market improvement can be expected in the short or medium term (Art. 2).

An obligation is imposed on the Commission to collect (and member states to supply) data and to monitor the market so as to detect a possible crisis (Art. 3). Where a crisis exists, at the request of a member state the Commission may introduce restrictive measures to prevent any increase in the activities of existing undertakings or to restrict access to the market to new entrants. Such measures remain valid for not more than six months, a period which can only be extended once by a further six months (Art. 4(4)).

Hired vehicles (Directive 84/647)

In order to facilitate the use of motor vehicles hired without drivers for road haulage, Directive 84/647 was adopted harmonizing national laws. The Directive does not affect national laws which lay down less restrictive conditions (Art. 4), nor such matters as, for example, prices and conditions for road haulage (Art. 5). However, the Directive does require member states, under certain conditions, to allow motor vehicles hired by undertakings established in other member states to be used on their territory for the purpose of road haulage. The conditions that can be demanded are: the motor vehicle must be registered in compliance with the laws of the member state where it was hired; the contract solely relates to the hiring of a motor vehicle without a driver; and the hired vehicle must be used only by the undertaking concerned and driven only by the staff of that undertaking. As proof of the above conditions, two documents, the contract of hire and, where the person driving the motor vehicle is not the person hiring the vehicle, the driver's contract of employment, must be carried on board (Art. 2).

Own-account operations carried out by vehicles weighing more than 6 tonnes may be excluded from the scope of the Directive (Art. 3(2), as amended). A proposal for a new Directive in this field has been withdrawn.

Road transport (passengers)

Current status

In the sector of passenger transport progress has been rather slow and is currently governed by Regulation 684/92,[15] substantially amended by

---

[15] OJ 1992 L 74/1, as amended, on common rules for the international carriage of passengers by coach and bus.

Regulation 11/98,[16] and by Commission Regulation 2121/98,[17] which laid down detailed rules for the application of Regulation 684/92 as regards documents for international carriage of passengers by coach or bus.

Background

Measures which have been adopted in this sector indicate a mixture of objectives which do not necessarily correspond to those of the measures adopted for goods haulage. There is more variety in the types of services provided for passengers.

In the 1960s and early 1970s measures were adopted concerning three types of services: occasional, regular and shuttle services. Regulation 117/66[18] introduced common definitions of these services and rules for international carriage of passengers by coach and bus where occasional services were provided, such as closed-door tours. Regulation 516/72[19] laid down common rules for shuttle services and Regulation 517/72[20] laid down common rules for regular services.

Once these two measures were adopted, the Community, as required by Regulation 117/66, extended the regime of common rules in respect of all passenger transport services to certain non-Community countries. In order to comply with the Regulation, the Council concluded in 1982 an Agreement on the International Carriage of Passengers by Road by means of Occasional Coach and Bus Services (ASOR – Accord Services Occasional Transport Routier)[21] with Austria, Spain, Finland, Norway, Portugal, Sweden, Switzerland and Turkey.[22] ASOR provides for a standard form of control documents and liberalization of certain types of occasional services. Although ASOR is part of Community law by virtue of Council Decision 82/505,[23] the Council adopted Regulation 56/83[24] in order to ensure proper implementation of ASOR. The Regulation covers such matters as who are the competent national authorities referred to in the agreement, who issues certain documents and who adopts implement-

---

[16] OJ 1998 L 4/1.

[17] OJ 1998 L 268/10 replacing Regulation 1839/92, OJ 1992 L 187/5, as from the end of 1999.

[18] JO 1966, p. 2688.

[19] OJ 1972 L 67/13.

[20] OJ 1972 L 67/19, amended by several Council Regulations.

[21] OJ 1982 L 230/39.

[22] Austria, Spain, Finland, Portugal and Sweden have now joined the European Community and so all measures taken by the Community apply automatically to them as well.

[23] OJ 1982 L 230/38.

[24] OJ 1983 L 10/1.

ing measures. Provision is also made for the exchange of information and consultation, revision of the agreement, etc.

Common rules (Regulation 684/92)

This Regulation repealed the earlier three regulations and thus a single measure now contains the common rules. The 1998 amendment simplified the definition of various international coach and bus services by abolishing the concept of shuttle service.[25] In addition it added a new Article, Art. 3a, providing for the issue of a Community licence drawn up in accordance with a harmonized model and issued under a swift and efficient administrative procedure. The rules are equivalent to those applied for road haulage licences. The amendment also strengthens the enforcement provisions.

Regulation 684/92 applies to 'the international carriage of passengers by coach and bus within the territory of the Community by carriers for hire or reward or own-account carriers established in a member state in accordance with its law, using vehicles which are registered in that member state and are suitable, by virtue of their construction and equipment, for carrying more than nine persons, including the driver, and are so intended, and to the movement of such vehicles empty in connection with such carriage' (Art. 1). A change of vehicle or a change of mode of transport for part of the journey does not affect the application of this measure.

As far as the carriage between a member state and a non-Community country (or vice versa) is concerned, the Regulation follows its equivalent for road haulage operations. The Regulation applies to the part of the journey on the territory of the member state of picking up or setting down, after the conclusion of the necessary agreements between the Community and the third country concerned (Art. 1(2)). Pending the conclusion of such agreements, provisions contained in bilateral agreements concluded between a member state and a non-Community country apply.

Any carrier for hire or reward shall be free to carry out transport services without discrimination as to nationality or place of establishment if three conditions are met. First, the carrier must be duly authorized to offer the service in the state of establishment. Secondly, the carrier must satisfy the conditions laid down in accordance with Community rules on the admission to the occupation of road passenger transport operation in national and international transport operation.[26] Thirdly, the carrier must meet legal requirements on road safety as far as the standards for drivers

---

[25] The Regulation was amended following a 1996 report (COM (96) 190) on its operation.
[26] Directive 96/26, OJ 1996 L 124/1, discussed below.

and vehicles are concerned (Art. 3(1)). Own-account carriers must meet the third condition and also be authorized in the state of establishment to undertake carriage by coach and bus in accordance with the market-access conditions laid down by national legislation (Art. 3(2)).

The types of services (regular, occasional and own-account) are defined (Art. 2, as amended by Regulation 11/98). Some types of service do not require authorization (Art. 4). These include 'special regular services', such as the carriage of workers between home and work and the carriage to and from the educational institution for school pupils and students (Art. 2(1.2)) and occasional services such as closed-door tour operations (Art. 2(3.1)). In addition, empty vehicles connected with these services do not need an authorization. Own-account carriers require certificates and not authorizations (Art. 4(5)).

The common rules for the services which are subject to authorizations are set out in Arts 5 to 10. Authorizations are to be issued by national competent authorities of the member state in whose territory the place of departure is situated (Art. 6) and must conform to a common model drawn up by the Commission. A precise but tight timetable is set for agreement to be reached among all member states in whose territories passengers are picked up and set down (Art. 7).[27] Authorizations must not exceed five years (Art. 5(2), as amended).

Authorizations are issued in the name of the transport undertaking but, with consent from the competent authority, the service may be operated through a sub-contractor. The name of the sub-contractor shall be indicated in the authority. The sub-contractor must also fulfil the same conditions which were required of the authorized carrier (Art. 5(1)). Authorizations have to specify the type of service, the route of the service including the place of departure and the place of destination, and the period of validity of the authority. In the case of regular services, the authorizations must also specify the stops and the timetable (Art. 5(3)).

Obligations are imposed on the operator of a regular service to take all measures, until the authorization expires, to guarantee a transport service that fulfils the standards of continuity, regularity and capacity. Furthermore, the operator has a duty to comply with other conditions laid down by the authorizing authorities (Art. 10).

Those occasional services exempt from authorization are to be carried out under cover of a journey form and a set of translations of the journey form (Art. 11(1) to (3)). Details of the information required on the journey form are set out in the Regulation (Art. 11(4) to (6)).

---

[27] Where agreement is not reached Art. 7(6) permits a referral to the Commission.

As far as exempted own-account road passenger transport operations are concerned, they shall be subject to a system of certificates issued by competent authorities of the member state in which the vehicle is registered and shall be valid for the entire journey including transit. The certificates must conform to a model determined by the Commission (Art. 13).

The Regulation also details the information on transport tickets which passengers using regular services need to have (Art. 14). Authority is granted for authorized inspecting officers to be presented upon request with the authorization or journey form which includes the contract or certified true copy of it for 'special regular services' which do not require authorization under Art. 4(2) (Art. 15). The officers are also empowered to check the books and other documents, make copies or take extracts, have access to the undertakings' premises, sites and vehicles and to require the production of any information contained in books, documentation or databases (Art. 15(2)).

Mutual assistance between member states is mandatory in respect of information concerning breaches of relevant Community law committed in their own territory by a carrier from another member state and the penalties imposed as well as information on penalties imposed on their own carriers for breaches committed in another member state's territory (Art. 16(5)). Furthermore, the competent authorizing authority has a duty to withdraw an authorization if the holder no longer meets the conditions and, in particular, to ensure a carrier is prohibited from operating an international passenger service if the carrier repeatedly commits serious breaches of regulations governing road safety (Art. 16(1) to (3)).

Implementing measure (Commission Regulation 2121/98)
The substantial amendment to Regulation 684/92 required a similar updating exercise in respect of documents for the carriage of passengers by coach and bus. Regulation 2121/98 requires conformity with models provided in annexes for all documentation. The main control document is a journey form issued in books of 25 forms made out in the name of the carrier (Arts 1 and 2(1)). The journey form must be filled out legibly (Art. 2(2)) and be presented on demand to any enforcement official (Art. 6). A copy of the journey form must be kept on the vehicle during the whole of the journey and another at the undertakings' premises (Art. 2(2) and (3)). Slightly different rules apply for occasional services provided by non-resident hauliers within a member state (Art. 4).

The Regulation also sets out details required in applications for authorization, the authorizations themselves and certificates. Conformity with the models set out in Annexes III to V is mandatory (Arts 7 to 9).

Railways

Current status

The key legislative measures regulating this mode of transport are Directive 91/440[28] on the development of the Community's railways, Directive 95/18[29] on the licensing of railway undertakings and Directive 95/19[30] on allocation of infrastructure capacity and the charging of infrastructure fees. An evaluation of the operation of Directive 91/440 has concluded that there is a need to provide better access to rail infrastructure since very few undertakings have exploited their access rights. The Council has adopted, in March 2000, common positions on a railway 'package' of measures. The package consists of Directives amending Directive 91/440 and widening the scope of Directive 95/18, and a Directive to replace Directive 95/19.[31]

Background

After a hesitant start the Community finally started the real work of liberalizing the rail transport sector in the late 1980s. The 1989 Communication entitled 'EC Railways Strategy'[32] was the springboard for action. One of the major difficulties in opening up access to the railway market and providing an internal market in rail services at Community level has been the issue of infrastructure ownership. Unlike other transport modes, railway undertakings offer transport services and in the process they use an infrastructure they own. This hinders the development of trans-frontier services and provides unequal treatment between the various modes in respect of infrastructure costs.

During the 1990s there was much debate on the future of the Community's railways as well as the adoption of important legislative measures such as Directive 91/440 which initiated the liberalization of rail transport. In 1996 the Commission issued a White Paper entitled *A Strategy for Revitalising the Community's Railways*.[33] This document analyses a number of problems facing the railways and also suggests a number of ways to revitalize the sector. The Commission's vision for a future railway system is based on the following objectives: to ensure the economic independence of the national railways; to open access to

---

28 OJ 1991 L 237/25.
29 OJ 1995 L 143/70.
30 OJ 1995 L 143/75.
31 COM (1999) 616 final, Vols. I–III.
32 OJ 1990 C 34/8.
33 COM (96) 421 final which took as its basis the report of an advisory group set up by the Commission. The report is entitled *The Future of Rail Transport in Europe*.

Europe's rail networks; to clarify the divisions of responsibility between the state and the railways; and to bring together the national railway systems. These measures should be supported by the Community in providing a modernized regulatory framework, as well as measures for integrating national systems at European level such as establishing corridors or 'freight freeways' across Europe. Thus railways will be able to match the speed and reliability of road hauliers. The proposals have resulted in much debate in the member states.

Access to national infrastructures (Directive 91/440 (Article 10))
The aim of this measure is to facilitate the adaptation of the Community's railways to the needs of the Single Market and to increase the industry's efficiency (Art. 1). This is to be achieved by laying down four basic rules for railway organization: independent management, sound finances, financial separation of infrastructure management and transport operations; and certain rights of access to national railway infrastructure. The latter, set out in Art. 10, is granted to international groupings of railway undertakings operating freight services and to railway undertakings engaged in the international combined transportation of freight.[34]

International groupings are granted transit rights but only for services between member states. In order to qualify as an international grouping the association must have at least two railway undertakings established in different member states for the purpose of providing international transport services between member states (Art. 3). Furthermore, member states may exclude from the scope of the Directive railway undertakings which provide only urban, suburban or regional services (Art. 2(2)).

Although this Directive has partially opened up the market by permitting some railway undertakings to operate trains on the same tracks as incumbent rail operators, it has not been an enormous success. The scope of the Directive is further limited by the fact that the implementation of the rules for determining the conditions under which other undertakings have access to the market and the conduct of their businesses remain in the hands of the national railway bodies who are often the competitors (Art. 10(2) and (3)).

In 1998 a Commission Communication was published on the implementation and impact of the Directive with particular reference to access rights for rail freight.[35] The report confirmed that further action is necessary to

---

[34] Passenger services do not come within the scope of this measure.
[35] COM (98) 202 final.

define the conditions of market access. The proposed amendment to Art. 10, however, is not far reaching. It is proposed to allow individual operators to come within the scope of the Directive and to extend the scope of Art. 10 to include access to international freight services operating on a defined European network (i.e. Trans-European Rail Freight Networks).

Community rail licence (Directive 95/18)
This measure lays down rules which determine who is a railway undertaking and introduces rail transport licences (recognized as valid throughout the Community) for all railway undertakings providing services referred to in Art. 10 of Directive 91/440. The Directive expressly excludes operators providing urban, suburban and regional services as well as international groupings the activity of which is limited to providing shuttle services through the Channel Tunnel (Art. 1).

Each member state is obliged to designate a licensing authority to carry out the obligations imposed by this Directive. The licensing authority must be independent and must not provide rail transport services itself (Art. 3). In order to obtain a licence an operator must apply to the licensing authority in the member state in which it is established (Art. 4(1)) and meet certain requirements in relation to good repute, financial fitness, professional competence[36] and cover for its civil liability in case of accidents (Arts 5 to 9).

The national licensing authority must make public its procedures for granting a licence and respond to an application quickly and not more than three months after receiving all relevant documentation. A refusal to grant a licence must be justified and subject to judicial review (Art. 15). The licence remains valid as long as the undertaking concerned fulfils the obligations set out in the Directive but the licensing authority may require regular review at least every five years (Art. 10). Licensing authorities may withdraw the licence immediately where there is serious doubt about the undertaking's compliance with the Directive (Art. 11). In addition, the Directive requires the undertakings to comply with national law compatible with Community law in respect of technical, safety and social regulations (Art. 12).

Allocation of infrastructure capacity (Directive 95/19)[37]
The granting of a licence under Directive 95/18 does not necessarily pro-

---

[36] The conditions relating to professional competence (Art. 8) will be strengthened by a non-discriminatory treatment requirement.
[37] This Directive is likely to be replaced by the end of 2000. See n. 31.

vide access to all the infrastructure capacity needed to run a train between two places at a given time as the licensed operator might desire. Thus Directive 95/19 was adopted to regulate the allocation of infrastructure capacity among licensed undertakings and the charging of infrastructure fees in a uniform manner throughout the Community (Art. 1).[38]

Each member state has to appoint an allocation authority responsible for allocating rail capacity on an equitable and non-discriminatory basis ensuring the allocation procedure is enforced effectively (Art. 3). The Directive, however, permits the national allocation authority to prioritize public services and services provided on a specific railway infrastructure such as high-speed lines and freight lines (Arts 4 and 5).

Procedures for allocation of capacity are laid down by member states and published (Art. 10(1)). An application must be submitted to the allocation authority of the member state in the territory which the departure point of the service concerned is situated. The allocation authority to which an application has been submitted shall inform other relevant allocation authorities of the request. These latter authorities have a maximum of one month to take a decision. The allocation authority to which an application has been submitted shall, together with other relevant allocation authorities, take a decision in not later than two months. In both cases the time period runs from the moment all relevant information has been submitted. Once the licence has been granted, the undertaking concerned will conclude administrative, technical and financial agreements directly with the infrastructure manager (Art. 10).

Member states shall also provide that a safety certificate, in which the railway undertakings' safety requirements are set out, be submitted in order to ensure safe service on the routes concerned. In order to obtain the safety certificate, the railway undertakings must comply with certain regulations under national law as long as they are compatible with Community law.

Member states are obliged to ensure decisions are open to appeal before an independent body whose own decisions are subject to judicial review (Art. 13).

Member states may demand a deposit or similar security from the applicant when submitting an application for infrastructure access. If the undertaking does not make use of the allocated train path, an amount may be deducted from the deposit to cover costs incurred in processing the application and any subsequent loss of earnings due to the non-use of the infrastructure capacity (Art. 12).

---

[38] Infrastructure fees are discussed in Chapter 6.

Inland waterways

Current status

The main legislative measures ensuring access to the Community's inland waterways are Regulation 2919/85[39] laying down the conditions for access to the arrangements under the Revised Convention for the Navigation of the Rhine (the Mannheim Convention) to vessels belonging to the Rhine Navigation, Directive 82/714[40] on inland navigation certificates, Directive 76/135[41] on navigability licences and Regulation 1356/96[42] on common rules to establish freedom to provide such transport services.

As stated above, overcapacity has been a problem for this mode of transport. Regulation 718/99,[43] on a Community-fleet capacity policy to promote inland waterway transport, extended an exiting scrapping premium scheme until 2003.

Background

Most of the Community's inland waterway traffic is carried on the Rhine. Thus the main provisions governing the inland navigation sector are those relating to the Mannheim Convention and the Additional Protocol 2 signed in 1979 which amended the Convention. In order to incorporate these provisions into Community law the Council adopted Regulation 2919/85.

The Mannheim Convention

The six contracting states to the Mannheim Convention, that is, five member states of the European Community (Belgium, Germany, France, The Netherlands and the United Kingdom) and Switzerland agreed to maintain the general principle of free navigation of the Rhine and its mouth for the transport of goods or passengers (Art. 1).

Once the Community was established, it was necessary to ensure that the scheme governing the Rhine, the major waterway of the Community, would apply without discrimination to all the member states. In 1964 the Commission issued a Memorandum[44] on the application of the EC Treaty to the navigation of the Rhine. In the Memorandum the Commission out-

---

[39] OJ 1985 L 280/4.
[40] OJ 1982 L 301/1.
[41] OJ 1976 L 21/10.
[42] OJ 1996 L 175/7.
[43] OJ 1999 L 90/1. Commission Regulation 805/99, OJ 1999 L 102/64, lays down certain measures for implementing Regulation 718/99.
[44] COM (64) 140.

lined its view on the legal relationship between the Treaty of Rome and the Mannheim Convention.

The Additional Protocol to the Revised Convention (1979), signed by the six contracting states, states that only vessels belonging to the Rhine Navigation shall be authorized to transport goods and passengers on the Rhine waterway. Vessels are considered to belong to the Rhine Navigation if they carry a document, known as a certificate, issued by the competent authority (Art. 2(3) of the Convention).

The Protocol of Signature to the Additional Protocol provides that the certificate stating that a vessel belongs to the Rhine navigation shall be issued by the competent authority of the state concerned only to vessels which have a genuine link with that state. The factors considered in establishing such a link are to be determined on the basis of equal treatment between the contracting states to the Convention. Further, the Protocol provides that the same treatment must be accorded to vessels which have a genuine link with any EC member state. The other member states are, therefore, accorded equal status with the contracting states to the Convention.

A Central Commission for the Navigation of the Rhine (CCR), established in Strasbourg, was created in order to examine complaints resulting from the application of the Convention, as well as the execution of the agreed implementing provisions among the governments, and in order to rule on appeals against judgments rendered before the inferior courts for the navigation of the Rhine. Within the CCR the contracting states to the Convention then drew up implementing provisions determining the conditions under which these certificates should be issued.

These implementing provisions were incorporated into Community law in the following manner. First, the Council adopted a decision deferring the common action required of those member states which are contracting parties to the Convention when agreeing on the CCR's resolution adopting these implementing provisions. Secondly, in order to ensure that these implementing provisions were put into effect throughout the Community, the Council adopted Regulation 2919/85, laying down the conditions for access to the arrangements under the Revised Convention for the navigation of the Rhine relating to vessels belonging to the Rhine Navigation.

Access of member states to the navigation of the Rhine (Regulation 2919/85)
The Regulation has two objectives. First, to set the conditions under which member states, other than those contracting states to the Mannheim Convention, have equal access to the navigation of the Rhine. Secondly, to prevent nationals or undertakings from non-Community countries from

establishing themselves in a contracting state and profiting in that way of the freedom of navigation.

The Regulation therefore sets out in an annex the procedures which member states have to follow in respect of the document certifying that a vessel belongs to the Rhine Navigation, provided for in the third paragraph of Art. 2 of the Revised Convention for the Navigation of the Rhine. It seeks to ensure that only vessels with a genuine link with a member state are eligible.

The authorities of the member state in which a vessel is registered in a public register are alone competent to issue and withdraw certificates. Where no public register exists, or in the event of a vessel not being registered in a member state, the member state in which the owner of the vessel (or, in the case of joint ownership, the first joint owner to apply for the document) has his domicile, usual residence or registered office, shall be competent to issue, cancel or withdraw the certificate (Art. 2 of the annex).

The certificate shall not be issued for a vessel unless the owner of that vessel, be it a natural or legal person, governed by public or private law, is a national of or established in a member state and has their domicile, residence or registered office in that state. In cases in which the owner is a legal person governed by private law, in addition to the above requirements, the owner's principal place of business, that is, the place from which the vessel operates, must be in that member state. Further, the majority of its management must be composed of Community nationals (Art. 3).

A member state may, exceptionally, after consulting the CCR, grant derogations from some of these requirements on condition that the objective of Additional Protocol 2 is not endangered. The CCR may establish the general conditions under which these derogations will be granted.

The operator of a vessel must also fulfil the same conditions as the owner in order to obtain the certificate for the vessel which he is operating (Art. 5). This can be issued by the member state where the operator has his domicile or usual residence, or in which the registered office of the undertaking is situated.

The certificate must state the name, number, place of registration, type and category of the vessel as well as the name, business name, domicile, usual residence or registered office of the owner and, where appropriate, of the operator. The certificate must be kept on board the vessel and must be produced, on demand, to the inspecting authorities.

Inland navigation certificates (Directive 82/714)
This Directive was adopted pursuant to Art. 7 of Directive 76/135 (see below), which established technical requirements for inland waterway

vessels. Directive 82/714 provides for a Community inland navigation certificate valid on all Community waterways except those not linked to the waterways of other member states and those where the Revised Convention for the Navigation of the Rhine applies. The Directive provides for the classification of the Community inland waterways into 'Zones 1, 2, 3 and 4' (each of which is determined in Annex 1 of the Directive), as well as Zone R which is covered by the Revised Convention (Art. 1).

The scope of this measure is limited to certain size vessels, tugs and pusher crafts and it does not apply to passenger vessels (Art. 2) which fall under the scope of Directive 76/135.

Vessels operating on the Community waterways of all zones must carry one of two certificates (Art. 3). When operating on a Zone R waterway a certificate issued pursuant to Art. 22 of the Revised Convention is required. This certificate will grant access to all Community waterways subject, in certain cases, to the possession of a supplementary Community certificate (Art. 4). Member states are permitted in view of their local importance and special safety requirements to exempt from the application of the whole or part of this Directive certain vessels which do not operate on the inland waterways of other member states (Art. 7). When operating solely in waterways of other zones it is sufficient to have a Community inland navigation certificate issued to vessels complying with technical requirements for those zones.

The certificate attests to the compliance of vessels with common technical requirements. Directive 76/135 remains applicable to those vessels covered by it which are not covered by this Directive, such as passenger vessels.

The Community certificate is issued by member states in which the vessel is registered or, failing that, the member states in which its home port is situated or, failing that, of the member state in which the owner is established (Art. 9). A certificate may be issued to a vessel laid down as from 1 January 1985 following a technical inspection carried out prior to the vessel being put into service and intended to check whether the vessel complies with technical requirements of the Directive (Art. 8(1)). The certificate is valid for a period not exceeding ten years (Art. 11).

The competent authorities are to carry out the technical inspection which can nevertheless be avoided by producing a valid attestation, issued by a classification society approved by the state in which the certificate is issued, that the vessel satisfied in whole or in part the technical requirements of the Directive (Art. 10).

Any decision to refuse to issue or renew the Community certificate shall be reasoned and an appeal procedure provided. A valid certificate may be withdrawn if the vessel ceases to comply with the technical requirements specified in the Directive (Art. 16).

Member states may recognize the navigability certificates of vessels from non-Community countries and, where appropriate, issue Community certificates or supplementary Community certificates to vessels from such countries (Art. 18).

Navigability licences (Directive 76/135)

Since the adoption of Directive 82/714 this measure remains only partly applicable. It applies to certain categories of vessels listed in Art. 8(2) of Directive 82/714, passenger vessels and vessels which carry a Community certificate but do not yet comply with the requirements of Directive 82/714 (Art. 20 of Directive 82/714).

Navigability licences are issued by the member state in which the vessel is registered or has its home port or, failing that, by the member state in which the owner of the vessel is domiciled (Art. 2(2)). Each member state must recognize for navigation on its national waterways the navigability licences issued by another member state (Art. 3), on condition that the licence was issued or last extended not more than five years previously and has not expired.

Common rules for access (Regulation 1356/96)

The Regulation lays down the common rules under which a carrier may transport goods or persons by inland waterway between member states and in transit through them. The Regulation does not apply to cabotage and does not affect the rights of non-Community operators obtained under the Revised Rhine Convention (Art. 3).

Any operator shall be allowed to carry out inland waterway transport operations without discrimination on grounds of nationality or place of establishment if certain conditions are met. First, the operator must be established in a member state. Secondly, the operator must be entitled to carry out the international transport of goods or persons by inland waterway. Thirdly, the operator must use vessels which are registered in a member state, or in the absence of registration, possess a certificate of membership of a fleet of a member state. Fourthly, the conditions laid down in Regulation 3921/91 under which non-resident carriers may transport goods or persons by inland waterway within a member state (see below) must be satisfied (Art. 2).

Structural overcapacity (Regulation 718/99)

The main concern in this sector was the need for structural improvements due to the over-capacity in the fleets operating on the linked inland waterway networks of Belgium, France, Germany, Luxembourg and the Netherlands, which strongly affected the economics of the carriage of goods by this mode of transport. This problem was partly resolved by the implementation of Regulation 1101/89,[45] which has been replaced by Regulation 718/99.

The 1989 Regulation provided for the reduction of the fleet overcapacity through vessel scrapping actions coordinated at Community level. Regulation 718/99 aims to maintain the market regulation mechanism currently in force, the 'old-for-new' rule until 2003. This will prevent the effects of the scrapping actions carried out in the 1990s from being wiped out by bringing into service of new capacity just after the expiry of the 1989 Regulation. Thus, during this period, the owner of a cargo-carrying vessel to be brought into service must either scrap tonnage (without receiving a scrapping premium) in line with the ratio between old and new tonnage set by the Commission, or pay a special contribution (a premium) into the Inland Waterways Fund covering the vessels. The ratio may be set at different levels for different sectors of the market but it will be constantly reduced to bring it quickly and in regular stages to zero over the four-year period (Art. 4). After 2003 the tonnage regulatory mechanism will be transformed into a surveillance mechanism which will enable the 'old-for-new' rule to be reactivated, but only in the event of a serious market crisis, and if necessary, to accompany it with structural improvement measures (Art. 6).

The Inland Waterways Fund is to be operated by competent authorities of the member states concerned as stated in the Regulation (Art. 3).

Tariffs

Inland transport (general)

Current status

Two important legislative measures, common to all inland modes of transport, were adopted in the 1960s. They are Regulation 11 concerning the abolition of discrimination in transport tariffs and conditions[46] and Regulation 1191/69 on the concept of 'public service' obligations.[47]

Background

Measures on transport tariffs and conditions are designed to prevent the abuse of dominant position and the development of cut-throat competi-

---

[45] OJ 1989 L 116/25.
[46] JO 1960 p. 1121 (plus Commission Recommendation to member states on the application of Regulation 11, JO 1961 p. 975.
[47] OJ 1969 L 156/1, subsequently amended.

tion. The structure of the Community's tariff system for inland transport is governed by Arts 75 and 76 of the EC Treaty. These Arts seek to abolish discrimination in tariffs and conditions for transporting freight on grounds of country of origin or of destination of goods and tariff support respectively (notably no reference is made to the transporting of passengers). Article 75 prohibits discrimination where individual transport undertakings are concerned. Article 76 specifically prohibits member states providing tariff support in favour of undertakings unless authorized by the Commission.

Prohibition of discrimination (Regulation 11)
The Regulation applies to the transport of goods by road, rail and inland waterways within the Community and also between member states and third countries. However, the Regulation only applies to those sections of the journey that take place within the Community and only to the sections of the journey where the means of transport are road, rail or inland waterways. When goods are transported by successive carriers under a single contract, the Regulation applies to each carrier only for that section of the journey which he performs. The Regulation provides that discrimination by charging different tariffs and imposing different conditions for carrying the same goods over the same transport links, on grounds of country of origin or of destination of goods, shall be prohibited. Further, the fixing of transport tariffs and conditions which, when applied, would constitute discrimination, is also prohibited. Transport undertakings and governments have an obligation to supply information that the Commission may request concerning tariffs or other agreements on rates and conditions (Art. 11). Where a carrier sets different tariffs or imposes different conditions for applying the same goods over the same routes he must be prepared to rebut the presumption that this is an infringement of the Regulation (Art. 12). Different tariffs may be set and different conditions imposed if this results solely from competition between carriers or is due to operating conditions. For example, in the rail sector there is often a duty to accept passengers or goods at certain tariffs and subject to certain conditions. The tariffs are fixed by the governmental authority and unprofitable to the carrier but are so imposed by the 'public service obligation' that the operators are requested to perform.

The Commission has the power to investigate any cases of discrimination in transport tariffs and conditions. It does so either on its own initiative or if so requested by a member state. Following its investigation it may issue a decision in which it determines whether discrimination has occurred. Prior to taking this decision the Commission must consult the member states directly concerned but such a consultation is more in the nature of exchange of views rather than a hearing. The Commission's decision may include advice to the member state concerned on any remedial action that may be necessary. Member states are required to lay down appropriate penalties for carriers who do not comply with the requirements. The Commission may itself impose fines on undertakings which do not supply information requested or supply information which they know to be false. Where the Commission has decided that discrimination exists it may impose fines not exceeding 20 times the price of carriage. Where discrimination persists, despite the Commission's decision, the Commission may impose a penalty for each instance of discrimination. The Commission must, however, consult the member state(s) concerned before imposing the penalty. It must also notify the undertaking concerned of its intention to impose a fine and, before coming to a decision, it must give the undertaking concerned an opportunity to be heard. (These provisions have never been applied.)

Public service obligations (Regulation 1191/69)
This measure defines 'public service obligation' as including one of the following duties: the duty to operate according to published schedules regardless of the amount of traffic; the duty to provide transport of freight or passengers on reasonable routes to all users; and the duty to accept passengers and freight at certain rates and subject to certain conditions which may be non-commercial. Governments may require operators to continue to provide unprofitable services but indemnify them for losses sustained. The amount of compensation the undertaking will receive is to be equal to the difference between the reduced cost and the decrease in revenue if all or part of the service were to be terminated. The Regulation, however, provides for transport undertakings to apply to member states for permission to terminate any part of their services which results in 'economic disadvantages' (Art. 4). The member states may investigate the cause of the hardship and withhold compensation where the cause appears to be temporary, accidental, or where it can be remedied by a change in the operating methods.[48]

Road transport

Current status
Agreements between member states relating to international tariffs were abolished from 1 January 1990 by Regulation 4058/89.[49]

---

[48] Case 36/73 *Netherlands Railway Company of Utrecht v Netherlands Minister of Transport and Waterways* [1973] ECR 1299.
[49] OJ 1989 L 390/1, Art. 2.

Background

The Community's approach to the liberalization of tariffs was very similar to that of quotas. A series of Regulations were adopted, starting in 1968, establishing common rules on the rates for carriage of goods by road between member states.[50] The 1968 Regulation introduced a system of bracket tariffs which was replaced by more flexible systems in 1977 and 1983.

The system of bracket tariffs was questioned before the ECJ on the grounds that it conflicted with the objective of liberalizing trade and the establishment of a competitive economy within the Community.[51] The Court, however, ruled that the CTP could also have as an objective the balance of trade and fair competition and, in order to achieve these objectives, duties and restrictions might be imposed on transport undertakings.

Single tariff system (Regulation 4058/89)

The Regulation replaces all compulsory bracket rates and reference tariffs by a single tariff system for the entire Community. Rates are to be set by free agreement between the parties to the haulage contract (Art. 2), although professional carriers' organizations may recommend rates. With a view to monitoring the market, the Regulation also provides for member states to request any information concerning the rates charged from the various parties concerned with international carriage of goods by road (Art. 3(1)). Any such information is covered by the obligation of professional secrecy.

Railways

Current status

The legislative measures regulating railway rates are Regulation 2183/78 laying down uniform costings principles for railway undertakings,[52] Decision 82/529 on the fixing of rates for freight[53] and Decision 83/418 in respect of international passenger and luggage traffic.[54]

Background

Railways, more than any other mode of transport, have been heavily regulated by the member states. Although Art. 75 EC Treaty and Regulation 11

---

[50] Regulations 1174/68, OJ 1968 L 194/1; 2831/77, OJ 1977 L 334/22; 3568/83, OJ 1983 L 359/1, subsequently amended.

[51] Case 12/82 *Ministère Public v Trinon* [1982] ECR 4089.

[52] OJ 1978 L 258/1.

[53] OJ 1982 L 234/5.

[54] OJ 1983 L 237/32.

abolished discrimination in transport rate and conditions, railway undertakings are not totally free to set their own rates. One of the main obstacles to progress has been the organization and administration of railways. The rail industry is a special sector, which does not lend itself to the same treatment as other modes of transport. The duty to accept passengers or freight at certain rates and subject to certain conditions is often imposed by governmental authority by virtue of public service obligations.

Uniform costing principles (Regulation 2183/78)

The aim of this measure is to ensure closer cooperation between the main railway undertakings and to improve their financial situation. The Regulation applies only to national railway undertakings and lays down uniform costing principles but only for international freight transport carried in 'full train loads' (Art. 1(1)). Thus the consignment must comprise several wagon loads offered for carriage at the same time by the same sender at the same station and forwarded direct as a full train to the same consignee at the same destination station (Art. 1(3)).

The main principle is that railway undertakings are to calculate the *change* in their total costs resulting from the introduction of new traffic, from an increase or a reduction in existing traffic or from the termination of such traffic.

For new traffic, or for an increased volume of existing traffic, 'change' means the additional costs to the undertaking resulting from the acceptance of such traffic. For existing traffic the termination of which is considered, or for a reduction in volume of existing traffic, 'change' means the saving costs resulting from the termination or reduction of such traffic (Art. 3(1)).

The Regulation also provides a standard list of factors to be taken into consideration in calculating costs, such as terminal services, maintenance of motive power, maintenance and replacement (or depreciation) of safety and telecommunications installations, etc. (Annex I). Further, certain elements are to be taken into account when calculating costs, such as the characteristics of the traffic in question and all movements and operations associated with such traffic (Annexes II and III).

Rates for international freight (Council Decision 82/529)

The Decision, which also applies to national railway undertakings, states that the fixing of tariffs and conditions for international freight transport between member states must be done by the undertakings themselves in accordance with their commercial interests and taking account of the cost price and the market conditions (Art. 2). These tariffs must be published (Art. 8). The Decision recognizes this will only be achieved when sufficient commercial independence in the management of undertakings is achieved (Art. 5).

The rates are to be drawn up in the form of common tariffs scales offering rates for the whole journey or tariffs consisting of the sum of the rates obtained from scales applicable on the sections of the railway networks concerned (Art. 3(2)). Special agreements may be concluded between undertakings and customers designated by name. They shall contain rates which take account of conditions of a technical and commercial character peculiar to the type of transport involved (Art. 6).

Rates for international passenger and baggage traffic (Council Decision 83/418)
The Decision concerns the commercial independence of railway undertakings in the management of their international passenger and luggage traffic. It states that undertakings are free to establish common tariff scales offering rates for the whole journey, to offer all-in package services, to create revenue pools and to delegate powers among themselves to make joint offers to customers (Art. 3). Thus undertakings are to operate international traffic along commercial lines.

Inland waterways

Current status
Directive 96/75[55] sets out common Community provisions for chartering and pricing in national and international inland waterway transport.

Background
Different national laws impeded the smooth functioning of the internal market in this sector. The laws were concerned with systems of chartering by rotation, namely a system which consists of allocating in a charter exchange requests for transport operations, at previously fixed prices and under conditions made known, from customers on the basis of the order in which vessels became available after unloading. Carriers were asked, in order of their registration on the rota,[56] to choose in turn a load from those on offer. Those who made no choice nonetheless kept their position in the order.

---

[55] OJ 1996 L 304/12.

[56] The system worked by apportioning the demand from customers for capacity on board ship in strict rotating order among the boats which were registered by their owners on the official charter exchange, as they were unloaded in turn and became free. The system mainly operated in Belgium and The Netherlands, a market which accounts for a third of the EC inland waterways market.

Prior to 1964 only one measure had been adopted which had direct effect on the Rhine. This was Regulation 11,[57] which abolished national discrimination in carriers' charges. The problem was essentially one of jurisdiction. Regulation 11 recognized the authority of the Central Rhine Commission.

National and international rates (Directive 96/75)
The Directive provides that in the field of national and international inland waterway transport in the Community contracts shall be freely concluded between the parties concerned and prices freely negotiated (Art. 2). Limited derogations were permitted until 1 January 2000.

The Directive also provides for the Commission, at the request of a member state, to act in cases of serious disturbances in the inland waterway market (Arts 7 and 8).

Frontier controls

One of the major obstacles to achieving access to foreign markets has been the formalities which take place at frontiers, many of which concern primarily the goods being transported. However, member states were used to perform at frontiers the checks, verification and inspections relating to technical characteristics, authorizations and other documentation with which vehicles and inland waterway vessels had to comply.

Road and inland waterways

Current status
Regulation 4060/89[58] has eliminated, since July 1990, formalities performed at the frontiers between member states.

Background
Until 1990 the transport of goods within the Community was accompanied by a transit advice note (T1 declaration), showing the nature and weight of the goods, the name and address of the sender, the date, the place from which they were transported, the place to which they were to be delivered, the route to be taken or distance travelled and the frontier crossing points, if any.[59] The need for any controls or formalities over goods transported under TIR and ATA carnets at internal frontier crossings was

---

[57] See n. 46.
[58] OJ 1989 L 390/18, as amended by Regulation 3356/91, OJ 1991 L 318/1.
[59] Regulation 222/77, OJ 1977 L 38/1 on the Community transit, subsequently amended and now abolished by Regulation 2726/90, OJ 1990 L 262/1.

abolished on 1 January 1991 by Regulation 719/91,[60] which repealed earlier directives relating to these carnets.

Elimination of frontier formalities (Regulation 4060/89)
The Regulation prohibits controls (i.e. checks, inspections, verifications) taking place at the frontier between member states where they concern means of transport registered or put into circulation in a member state (Arts 1 and 3). Controls must be performed in a non-discriminatory fashion (random checks) throughout the national territory and not at the frontier.[61]

Regulation 3912/92[62] was adopted to regulate transport registered or put into circulation in a non-Community country. The Regulation applies to controls performed by member states pursuant to an international agreement and to Regulation 4060/89. Controls may continue to be carried out at the external borders of the Community but not at internal frontiers. Any further checks, verifications or inspections must be carried out throughout the member states' respective territories as part of the normal control procedures (Art. 3).

Technical barriers

These were significant barriers in the transport industry which required an intensive programme of harmonization. This matter is considered in Chapter 5.

Rights of non-resident undertakings

The right of a non-resident undertaking to operate in a member state without having to meet formalities imposed by the host state is known as 'cabotage'. There was much opposition to the grant of this right from national industries operating road, maritime and air services. In some countries, such as Germany, road hauliers operated regionally. They felt threatened by the Dutch road haulage industry which operates internationally.[63] As far as maritime and air transport services were concerned,

---

[60] OJ 1991 L 78/6.
[61] Regulation 474/90, OJ 1990 L 51/1, amending Regulation 222/77, OJ 1977 L 38/1 which established the Community transit procedure and now replaced by Regulation 719/91, OJ 1991 L 78/6.
[62] OJ 1992 L 395/6.
[63] The second Commission Report on the liberalization of road cabotage, published in February 2000, shows that the Benelux countries dominated the business with close to 59% of the market. The Netherlands alone accounted for 31.2%. However, the share of cabotage in the activities of international hauliers has not increased much, with the liberalization going from 0.2% in 1990 to 1% in 1997, just before total liberalization.

national undertakings had enjoyed a monopoly on coastal and intra-member state routes.

Road transport (goods)

Current status
The right of a non-resident haulier to provide services within a member state is now governed by Regulation 3118/93[64] but has been exercised partially since 1 July 1990 (cabotage quotas/authorizations introduced for the first time) [65] and fully since 1 July 1998 (1989 Regulation was annulled by the ECJ).[66] The delay in adopting the 1993 Regulation to replace the annulled measure was due in part to its adoption being linked to the member states reaching agreement on a common system of charges for lorries using Community roads.[67]

Background
The right of a non-resident haulier to provide services within a member state has caused much difficulty to implement, and the problems were only resolved in the 1990s. As late as 1989 the European Court of Justice, in *Lambregts Transportbedrijf v Belgium*,[68] reminded the Council of its failure to discharge its obligation under Art. 71 of the EC Treaty by not adopting proposals authorizing road cabotage. The case concerned a Dutch haulier who had set up offices in a caravan in order to obtain a road transport licence in Belgium. The ECJ ruled that a road haulier could not justify cabotage activities on the basis of the right to provide services under Art. 49 of the EC Treaty. According to the Court's ruling, cabotage is governed by specific legislative measures as required by Art. 71.

Road cabotage (goods) (Regulation 3118/93)
The Regulation provides for a road haulier who is the holder of a Community authorization to offer international transport services as provided by Regulation 881/92 to be entitled to provide national road haulage services in the domestic market of another member state without being

---

[64] OJ 1993 L 279/1, subsequently amended by Regulation 3315/94, OJ 1994 L 350/9. Commission Regulation 792/94, OJ 1994 L 92/13 laid down rules for the application of Regulation 3118/93 to road haulage operators on own account.

[65] Regulation 4059/89 OJ 1989 L 390/3 introduced cabotage authorizations on a quota basis, each valid for two months.

[66] Annulled on procedural grounds by the ECJ in Case C-65/90 *European Parliament v Council* [1992] ECR I-4593 but allowed to remain effective until the Council, after consulting the European Parliament, adopted new legislation.

[67] See Chapter 6 for further details.

[68] Case 4/88 [1989] ECR 2583.

required to have a registered office or to be established in that member state, as long as his activities are of a temporary nature (Art. 1(1)).[69] Own-account operators entitled to carry out road haulage operations in the member state of establishment are also permitted to carry out cabotage operations as defined in point 4 of the Annex to the First Council Directive[70] (Art. 1(4)). Commission Regulation 792/94[71] lays down detailed rules for the application of Regulation 3118/93 to road haulage operators on own account. The Regulation entitles undertakings in the member state of establishment, in accordance with that member state's legislation, to carry out road haulage operations on their own account, and to receive the cabotage authorizations under the same conditions as undertakings carrying out road haulage operations for hire or reward.

The Regulation provides for the gradual introduction of cabotage operations within the framework of Community cabotage quotas, culminating in the total abolition of quotas in 1998.[72]

Save as otherwise provided by Community regulations, the host member state's laws, regulations and administrative provisions in specified areas apply to the performance of cabotage operations (Art. 6(1)) under the same conditions as those which that member state imposes on its own nationals so as to prevent any open or hidden discrimination on grounds of nationality or place of establishment (Art. 6(3)). These specified areas relate to rates and conditions governing the transport contract, weights and dimensions of road vehicles, requirements relating to the carriage of certain categories of goods, driving and rest time and value added tax (VAT) on transport services. In addition, the technical standards of construction and equipment which vehicles carrying out cabotage operations must meet are all those laid down for vehicles put into circulation in international transport (Art. 6(2)).

---

[69] COM (98) 47 final – Report on the implementation of Regulation 3118/93 as required by Art. 11. The report shows that in 1998 hauliers from Benelux were the most active in the cabotage market.

[70] See n. 10.

[71] OJ 1994 L 92/13.

[72] The Community cabotage quota consisted of cabotage authorizations, each valid for two months, which were allocated amongst the member states in accordance with a table set out in the Regulation (Art. 2(3)). The Commission distributed cabotage authorizations to the member state of establishment whose competent authorities issued them to carriers in accordance with certain specifications (Art. 3). A book of record sheets in which transport operations undertaken under a cabotage authorization were recorded, had to be returned with the authorization to the competent authority which had issued the authorization within eight days of the expiry of the validity of the authorization (Art. 4). The national competent authorities were required regularly to communicate to the Commission the data concerning cabotage operations (Art. 5(1)).

The Regulation also provides for mutual assistance by member states (Art. 8(1)) and for empowering national competent authorities of the host member state to impose penalties for those non-resident carriers who commit infringements of the Regulation or other legislation, in their territory, during the cabotage operation (Art. 8(2)).

Road transport (passengers)

Current status

Cabotage for the carriage of passengers by coach and bus is governed by Council Regulation 12/98[73] and came into force in June 1999. The Regulation lays down the conditions under which non-resident carriers may operate road passenger transport services within a member state (cabotage). The Regulation provides, *inter alia*, for the introduction of cabotage for regular internal services (urban and suburban services are excluded). Commission Regulation 2121/98[74] lays down detailed rules as regards documents for the international carriage of passengers.[75]

Background

This Regulation replaced an earlier measure which had been annulled by the ECJ.[76] A report was published on the application of the cabotage Regulation during the period 1993–96.[77] The report concluded that the impact of cabotage on the national markets of the member states has been marginal and insignificant as operators concentrated their activities on the national market. Cabotage operations are carried out in particular in adjacent member states. The report suggests that bus and coach cabotage will remain relatively unimportant, in the medium term, by comparison with resident carriage operators.

Road cabotage (passengers) (Regulation 12/98)

The Regulation lays down the conditions under which non-resident carriers may operate national road passenger transport services within a member state (cabotage transport operations). Any carrier who operates these services and who holds a Community authorization as provided by Regulation 684/92 on common rules for the international carriage of passengers by coach or bus shall be permitted, under the conditions laid down by this Regulation and without discrimination on grounds of the carrier's

---

[73] OJ 1998 L 4/10.
[74] OJ 1998 L 268/10.
[75] See above, where this Regulation has already been considered.
[76] Regulation 2454/92, OJ 1992 L 251/1 was annulled on procedural grounds in Case C-388/92 *European Parliament v Council* [1994] ECR I-6.
[77] COM (99) 327 final.

nationality or place of establishment, temporarily, to operate these services in another member state without being required to have a registered office or other establishment in that member state (Art. 1).

The Regulation defines 'regular services', 'special regular services' and 'occasional services' which are permitted for cabotage operations (Art. 2). As far as regular services are concerned, cabotage transport cannot be performed independently of a regular international service (Art. 3(3)). In addition, urban and suburban services – meaning transport services meeting the needs of an urban centre or conurbation, and transport needs between it and the surrounding areas – are excluded from the scope of the Regulation (Art. 3(3)).

In the same manner as for road haulage cabotage operations, passenger operations are subject, save as otherwise provided in Community legislation, to the laws, regulations and administrative provisions in force in the host member state in relation to rates and conditions governing the transport contract, weights and dimensions of road vehicles, requirements relating to the carriage of certain categories of passengers (e.g. schoolchildren, children and persons with reduced mobility), driving and rest time, and VAT on transport services (Art. 4(1)). Cabotage transport operations of regular services, unless otherwise provided by Community legislation, shall be subject to existing laws, regulations and administrative provisions in force in the host member state regarding authorizations, tendering procedures, the routes to be operated and the regularity, continuity and frequency of services as well as itineraries (Art. 4(2)). Vehicles used for cabotage operations shall be subject to technical standards of construction and equipment laid down for vehicles put into circulation for international transport (Art. 4(3)). In all cases the application of the host member state national provision to non-resident carriers must be on the same conditions as those imposed on their own nationals. No hidden discrimination on grounds of nationality or place of establishment is permitted (Art. 4(4)).

As far as cabotage of occasional services are concerned, these shall be carried out under cover of a control document – the journey form – which must be kept in the vehicle and produced when requested by an authorized inspecting officer (Art. 6(1)). In the case of 'special regular services' the contract concluded between the carrier and the transport organizer or a certified true copy of the contract shall serve as the control document (Art. 6(4)). The journey forms need to be returned to the competent authority.

Similarly to the obligations on member states for road haulage cabotage, the competent authorities are required each quarter to communicate to the Commission specified data. The competent authority of the host member state shall send the Commission statistics in respect of regular services (Art. 7(2)).

The Regulation also provides for action to be taken in the event of serious disturbances of the internal transport market[78] in a given geographical area (part or all of the territory of a member state or member states) due to or aggravated by cabotage (Art. 9). The Commission, upon request from the member state may adopt safeguard measures for a period of six months, renewable once. An advisory committee assists the Commission in the preparation of a model for journey forms (Art. 10) and to advise the Commission where a member state requests safeguard measures to be adopted. Mutual assistance amongst member states is mandatory (Art. 11) in particular in respect of infringements and penalties imposed.

Railways

Amendments proposed to Directive 91/440 envisage its scope being extended to grant infrastructure access to individual operators established in the Community and to include domestic freight transport.[79]

Inland waterways

Current status

Regulation 3921/91[80] lays down the conditions under which non-resident carriers may transport goods or passengers by inland waterways within a member state as from 1 January 1993.[81]

Background

Most inland waterway traffic in the Community is carried out on the Rhine-Moselle waterway, where cabotage operations were already completely deregulated. Regulation 3921/91 does not affect the rights existing under the Revised Rhine Convention.

Inland waterway cabotage (Regulation 3921/91)

The Regulation permits temporary access to inland waterways of a member state to any carrier of goods or persons established in another member state and entitled to undertake international transport operations of goods and persons. Such a carrier will not be required to set up a registered office or other establishment in the member state whose waterways he intends to

---

[78] This means the serious and potentially enduring excess of supply over demand, a threat to the financial stability and survival of a significant number of road passenger transport undertakings.

[79] See above.

[80] OJ 1991 L 373/1.

[81] Germany and France were allowed to derogate from the provisions of the Directive until 1 January 1995. The Regulation also does not affect the rights under the Revised Convention for the Navigation of the Rhine (the Mannheim Convention).

use (Art. 1). However, such access is only permitted to carriers who use for this purpose only vessels owned by Community nationals or persons domiciled in the Community or by undertakings registered in the Community and whose majority holding belongs to Community nationals (Art. 2(1)). Provision exists for a member state exceptionally to derogate from the condition that the majority holding in the undertakings has to belong to Community nationals (Art. 2(2)).

Proof that the carrier complies with the above conditions is by way of a certificate issued by the member state where the vessel is registered or by the member state in which the owner is established (Art. 2(3)). For those vessels belonging to the Rhine Navigation, the certificate of access provided under Regulation 2919/85 is sufficient.

Cabotage operations are, as usual, subject to the laws of the host member state in matters concerning tariffs and conditions governing transport contracts and chartering and operating procedures as well as technical specifications for vessels, navigation and police regulations, navigation time and rest periods and VAT. The application of these laws must be without any discrimination on the grounds of nationality or place of establishment (Art. 3).

Removal of restrictions on access to the occupation of transport services operator

Road transport (goods and passengers)

Current status
Admission to the occupation of road haulage or road passenger transport operator and mutual recognition of diplomas, certificates and other evidence of formal qualifications intended for these operators including the right to freedom of establishment in national and international transport operations, is governed by Directive 96/26,[82] as amended by Directive 98/76.[83] Directive 96/26 codified earlier Directives (discussed below) into a single text. Directive 98/76 extended the scope of Directive 96/26 as well as strengthening the requirements of good repute, financial standing and professional competence.

Background
The process of harmonizing national conditions for the admission to the

---

[82] OJ 1996 L 124/1.
[83] OJ 1998 L 277/17.

profession of transport operator started in 1974 with the adoption of two Directives.[84] Directive 74/561[85] defined 'the occupation of road haulage operator' as 'the activity of any undertaking transporting goods for hire or reward by means of either a self-contained motor vehicle or a combination of coupled vehicles'. This definition was incorporated into Art. 1(2) of Directive 96/26 and was simplified by Directive 98/76, which deleted the words 'self-contained' and 'coupled'. Directive 74/562,[86] as amended, defined the occupation of road passenger transport operator as 'the activity of any undertaking operating, by means of motor vehicles so constructed and equipped as to be suitable for carrying more than nine persons – including the driver – and intended for that purpose, passenger transport services for the public or for specific categories of users against payment by the person transported or by the transport organiser' (now Art. 1(2) of Directive 96/26).

Directive 77/796[87] facilitated the exercise of the right of establishment in the Community for both types of operator by requiring member states to accept, as sufficient proof of good reputation and financial standing, documents issued to that effect by the competent judicial or administrative authority of the transport operator's country of origin or the country of establishment. Where no such document is issued by the appropriate authorities, a declaration on oath in specified circumstances may replace the required document.

Directive 89/438[88] amended Directive 77/796 by introducing a written examination to prove professional competence or a minimum of five years' professional experience.

Admission to the occupation of transport operator (Directive 96/26)
The Directive applies to undertakings meeting the definition of road haulage operator and road passenger transport operator. The Directive does not apply to road haulage undertakings operating vehicles or combination of vehicles not exceeding a payload of 3.5 tonnes nor vehicles carrying less than nine persons (including the driver). The 1998 amendment extended the scope of the Directive to certain categories of road haulage operations using low-tonnage vehicles (e.g. courier services) (Art.

---

[84] The Directives also had the effect of harmonizing the qualifications, thus ensuring that they are above a certain minimum level.
[85] OJ 1974 L 308/18, subsequently amended.
[86] OJ 1974 L 308/23.
[87] OJ 1977 L 334/37, subsequently amended.
[88] OJ 1989 L 212/101.

2(1) as amended). Where the road haulage undertaking is engaged exclusively in national transport operations with only a minor impact on the transport market (due to the nature of the goods carried or the short distance involved), member states, after consultation with the Commission, may exempt them from the provisions of this Directive. Similar exemption can be obtained for road passenger services carried out for non-commercial purposes with minor impact on the market (Art. 2(2)(a) and (3)). Where road haulage operators use vehicles the maximum weights of which are between 3.5 and 6 tonnes, the member state may, after informing the Commission, exempt from application of all or parts of this Directive undertakings engaged exclusively in local short-distance transport and having only a minor impact on the transport market because of the short distances involved (Art. 2(2)(b)).[89]

In order to qualify, three conditions must be satisfied: good repute; appropriate financial standing (for the undertaking); and professional competence (for the undertaking's transport manager) (Art. 3(1)). Member states may determine the conditions under which road haulage undertakings may operate (up to a maximum period of one year, with an extension for a maximum period of six months), in derogation from the requirements under the above three conditions, in special circumstances (Art. 4, e.g. in the event of death or physical incapacity of the natural person in the occupation of road transport operator). Member states may also, by exception to the basic rules, and in special cases, authorize a person not fulfilling the conditions of professional competence (i.e. possession of the skills in the specified subjects listed in an Annex to the Directive) to continue to operate a transport undertaking provided that he has at least three years' practical experience in the day-to-day management of the undertaking (Art. 4).

As far as good reputation is concerned, the Directive leaves it to the member states to determine, except that it provides a list of matters which will deprive a member state from finding that the undertaking concerned meets the conditions. These are: conviction of serious criminal offences (including offences of a commercial character); declarations of unfitness to pursue the occupation of road transport operator under any rules in force; and conviction of serious offences against the rules in respect of pay and employment conditions in the profession or in respect of drivers' driving and rest periods, the weights and dimensions of commercial vehicles, road

---

[89] For those undertakings engaged in the occupation of road haulage operator before 1 October 1999 by means of vehicles for which the maximum authorized weights are between 3.5 and 6 tonnes, they shall comply with the new amendments in respect of financial standing (Art. 3(3)) by 1 October 2001 (new Art. 5(3)(b)).

safety, vehicle safety, the protection of the environment and other rules concerning professional liability (Art. 3(2), as amended).

The financial standing requirement is met where sufficient resources to ensure proper launching and proper administration of the undertaking exist. The Directive lists a number of matters the national competent authority has to take into account in deciding whether the undertaking meets this condition (e.g. annual accounts, funds available, costs). The Directive specifies the amount of capital and reserves needed to meet this condition of at least EUR 9000 when only one vehicle is used and at least EUR 5000 for each additional vehicle (Art. 3(3), as amended).[90]

Professional competence is met where the undertaking is in possession of skills demonstrated by passing a compulsory written examination (which may be supplemented by an oral examination) in subjects listed in Annex I of the Directive. Member states may exempt those operators who have proof of at least five years' practical experience in a transport undertaking at management level provided such applicants sit a test, the arrangements for which shall be determined by the member states in accordance with the amended Annex I (Art. 3(4), as amended).

As for applicants intending to engage solely in national transport operations, member states may stipulate that the knowledge to be taken into consideration in order to establish professional competence shall cover only subjects relating to national transport (Art. 3(4)(e), added in 1998).

Decisions taken by member states under this measure must be reasoned. Member states have an obligation to withdraw the authorization where the conditions are no longer satisfied (Art. 6) and to inform the member state of registration where offences against the rules governing road transport are committed by non-resident operators. If a withdrawal of authorization takes place, the Commission is to be informed and will pass the necessary information to the member states concerned. The national competent authorities are to check regularly, at least every five years, that these three conditions are being met by the undertakings concerned (Art. 6(1), as amended).

As for mutual recognition of diplomas, certificates and other evidence of formal qualifications are concerned, the Directive incorporates the provisions of Directive 77/796 and its amendments introduced by Directive 89/438 already mentioned above (Arts 8 and 9).

---

[90] Amounts as per Directive 98/76, OJ 1998 L 277/17, amending Directive 96/26.

Inland waterways

Current status

Directive 87/540[91] provides access to the occupation of carrier of goods by waterway in national and international transport and on the mutual recognition of diplomas, certificates and other evidence of formal qualifications for this occupation. The Directive also covers safety and technical requirements, which will be examined in Chapter 5.

Background

Following the satisfactory results which were obtained through the implementation of Directive 74/561 on admission to the occupation of road haulage operator in national and international transport operations, and Directive 77/796 aiming at the mutual recognition of diplomas, certificates and other evidence of formal qualifications for goods haulage operators and road passenger transport operators, it was considered necessary to adopt a similar Directive for the inland navigation sector.

Admission to the occupation of inland waterway operator (Directive 87/540)

This Directive applies to natural persons or undertakings pursuing the occupation of carrier of goods by inland waterway for hire or reward, even if this occupation is not exercised on a regular basis. In addition, the meaning of 'undertaking' is expressly extended to cover groups or cooperatives of operators whose purpose is to obtain business from shipping agents for distribution among their members irrespective of whether such groups or cooperatives possess legal personality. The Directive, however, does not apply to transport on own account, to operators using vessels with capacity not exceeding 200 tonnes, and nor does it apply to ferries (Art. 2).

The condition of 'professional competence' must be satisfied in order to be an authorized carrier (Art. 3(1)). Professional competence exists when the carrier has reached the standard of competence accepted to the national competent authority in the subjects listed in the Annex to the Directive (Art. 3(2)). These subjects include knowledge of the rudiments of civil law and commercial, social and tax legislation; the commercial and financial management of an undertaking; access to the market; as well as technical standards and technical aspects of transport, including safety.[92]

A member state may, after consulting the Commission, exempt from the application of the Directive carriers operating exclusively on navigable

---

[91] OJ 1987 L 322/20.
[92] See the Annex of the Directive for more details.

waterways within their territory not linked to the waterway network of another member state (Art. 3(3)).

The Directive authorizes member states to lay down the conditions on which a transport undertaking may, by way of derogation from Art. 3(1), operate on a provisional basis for a specified period in the event of the death or physical or legal incapacity of the natural person pursuing the occupation of carrier (Art. 4(1)).

Provision is made for those who have not had at least three years' practical experience in the everyday management of the undertaking applying to be authorized even though they do not meet the conditions of professional competence within the meaning of the Directive (Art. 4(2)).

Similarly, natural persons who provide proof that, before 1 July 1990, they legally pursued in a member state the occupation of carrier of goods by waterway in national or international transport are exempt from the need to prove that they meet the conditions laid down in the directive in order to obtain the certificate (Art. 5).

Authorizations may be withdrawn where the conditions of professional competence, certified by the possession of a certificate, are no longer met, subject to allowing, where appropriate, sufficient time for the recruitment of a replacement (Art. 6(2)).

Under Art. 7 each member state is to recognize the certificates issued by the competent authorities of another member state as sufficient proof of professional competence. Likewise, where a member state imposes on its own nationals certain additional requirements as to good repute, absence of bankruptcy or financial standing, that state is to accept, as sufficient evidence, in respect of nationals of other member states, the documents (extracts from judicial records, or certificates issued by banks or by other bodies designated by that state, or equivalent documents issued by a competent judicial or administrative authority in the carrier's country of origin or prior establishment) showing that these conditions have been met, and which are recognized as such in the state of origin or prior establishment (Arts 8 and 9).

Concluding observations

Where measures such as Community licences or certificates are introduced by Regulation, the effect is immediate and uniform throughout the Community. However, where the objective of the measures is to approximate the laws of the member states, Directives are adopted which means that legislative action has to be taken by the member states before the effects of the Directive are felt throughout the Community. This may result in delay in some member states.

CHAPTER 4

Positive liberalization: access to the market for maritime and air transport

Introduction

As already stated in Chapter 1, maritime and air transport sectors are specifically identified in the EC Treaty for separate treatment. Maritime transport has a long and well-established history of world-wide regulation, while air transport, although of much more recent origin, is primarily international like maritime transport. International conventions have been negotiated and signed in respect of both sectors.

In opening up the maritime transport market the Community had to take into account the different maritime traditions of the member states. Some member states had a tradition of state-owned fleets or strong links between industry and government; others had adopted an essentially *laissez-faire* approach to shipping. Member states also had varying interests in types of transport within the sector. For some member states the development of short-sea shipping is a priority; others may focus on fostering their deep sea shipping, where their shipping undertakings are heavily involved in cross-trading. A Community policy had to be aware of these differences and take them into account. Thus, as far as this mode of transport is concerned, the first significant step towards liberalization was the adoption of the 1986 package of legislative measures, when all intra-Community trade except coastal shipping (cabotage) was opened up. This was followed with a 1989 package of 'positive' proposals to improve the operating conditions and competitiveness of Community shipping. These proposals were aimed at establishing a Community register ('EUROS') alongside national registers and at making the Community fleet more competitive. The EUROS proposal has been withdrawn, but the other proposals, which included such measures as port inspections and environmental protection, were eventually adopted. In the 1990s the Community concentrated on the adoption of measures that ensure that safety and environmental standards are maintained. The Community's policy is to seek a global open market with particular emphasis on multilateralism and world-wide competition rules.

The Community faced a different but equally difficult problem in air transport. The enormous expansion of this industry, in a relatively short period, and particularly in the provisions of international transport services, resulted in a vast web of agreements between states. The provision of air services was governed by national law, the Chicago Convention of 1944[1] and a network of bilateral agreements between governments whose main objective was to protect their national airlines from competition. The Chicago Convention provides the basic multinational framework of international civil aviation, while bilateral agreements are concerned with rules for flights such as routes to be flown, designation of airlines and the setting of tariffs.

The bilateral agreements were modelled on the 'Bermuda II' agreements between the USA and the UK. These agreements, based on the universally recognized right of a state to control its air space, contained provisions on: landing rights and routes that may be flown by carriers from both parties; the number of flights that may operate on these routes; capacities that may be employed; and how they may be shared. The fares charged by each of the carriers were also agreed, and the revenue of both airlines shared on a percentage. It was only at the end of 1987, 30 years after the signature of the EC Treaty, that the first package of liberalization measures was adopted by the Council to deregulate scheduled flights between member states. Throughout these years, however, developments in the air transport industry were substantial. First, there was a vast growth in non-scheduled services (charters) which are relatively free from regulation in respect of access to routes, fares and capacity. Secondly, one member state, the UK, pursued a policy of deregulation throughout the 1980s. Thirdly, in their bilateral intergovernmental agreements, member states began to liberalize scheduled flights, as for example, in 1984 when the UK and The Netherlands concluded an agreement enabling any airline, established in either country, to fly between the two states. Fares were to be determined by the country in which the flight originated. Fourthly, in 1978 the US government deregulated its air transport industry, thus spurring EC member states to follow.

Although the EC Treaty expressly excluded air transport services from the application of the transport rules until the Council decided otherwise, it was evident that this regulatory system was contrary to the spirit of the

---

[1] Convention on International Civil Aviation, United Nations Treaty Series, vol. 15, p. 296.

Treaty. The situation was aggravated by inter-lining agreements on capacity and revenue sharing and coordination of timetables by airlines. The applicability of the EC competition rules to air transport were in dispute and therefore prevented Community initiatives in this area. However, the turning point came with the ruling of the ECJ, in *Nouvelles Frontieres*,[2] that the EC competition rules also apply to air transport. Since 1987, Community policy has been to phase out the bilateral system in order to establish a genuine single market in civil aviation and to apply the EC competition rules to this sector.

Removal of restrictions on the international carriage of goods and passengers

As far as maritime transport is concerned, the main restrictions concerned cargo-sharing agreements negotiated by governments or private parties. The 1974 UN Code of Conduct for Liner Conferences regulates cargo-sharing by providing that the national shipping lines of each contracting state are entitled to a 40% share of the traffic, with 20% available for cross-traders (the 40:40:20 rule). This was found to be necessary because developing countries had enacted laws reserving certain cargo to national carriers, that is, to ships flying their flags. The fear of bilateral cargo-sharing agreements completely closing competition led the maritime nations to negotiate and sign the UN Liner Conference Code.

As far as air transport is concerned, relaxation, rather than removal, of restrictions over market entry and over tariffs was the essence of the Community's policy, with an overriding concern to maintain safety. The Community dealt with access in three stages. First, legislation was adopted liberalizing scheduled inter-regional air services.[3] For the first time the industry was given a procedure for authorization which was not dependent on bilateral agreements between the parties' governments. Secondly, in the 1987 Civil Aviation Package included measures to improve market access. Although these measures were a major initiative, they did not go far enough and the expected reduction in fares and increase in competition did not materialize. Thus, thirdly, two further Civil Aviation Packages were agreed in 1989 and 1992 providing a much simpler procedure for access to all types of air services and the elimination of all intra-Community services for capacity control. The third package of measures for internal liberalization makes up the core of the *acquis communautaire* in air transport. The

---

2   Case 209-13/84 *Ministère Public v Lucas Asjes* [1986] ECR 1425.
3   Directive 83/416, OJ 1983 L 237/19, amended by Directive 89/463, OJ 1989 L 226/14.

package comprises three regulations, all of which cover scheduled and non-scheduled passenger and cargo services and relate to both international and domestic operations in the EC.

In 1993 the Commission set up a committee of 'Wisemen' to reflect and advise on the future of the industry. In its report[4] the committee, *inter alia*, identified a need for harmonization in the field of air traffic control, taxation, aircraft certification and pilot licences, as part of a wider cost-cutting exercise. On tax harmonization they recommended a considerable reduction in taxes and charges, advised against a carbon tax and supported a continued zero rate of VAT on international flights within the European Community. The aviation experts also prompted the Council to introduce a common external policy on transport. The Commission responded with a Communication[5] recognizing the obstacles to achieving a single market and outlining the Commission's strategy to achieve such a market by 1997.

The Commission's approach to the liberalization of the air transport market was one of tolerance rather than radical reform. Thus at first the Commission adopted regulations exempting certain common anti-competitive airline practices from the full effect of the application of the EC competition rules. Thus, for example, revenue pooling by which airlines share the income from a particular route, was exempted. Similarly, block exemption regulations were adopted to cover agreements on tariffs for passengers and cargo and slot allocation (times for take-off and landing granted to airlines). Protection for these practices was reduced as each package of liberalizing measures was adopted. The revenue pooling exemption was not renewed and measures were eventually adopted to govern the allocation of slots and to ensure that fares are freely negotiated. The rules have to be understood in conjunction with the relevant competition rules (see Chapter 7). A Commission Communication[6] was published in 1996 on the impact of the third package of air transport-liberalizing measures assessing the progress so far and outlining further action.

Freedom to provide maritime and air services

Maritime transport

Current status

Regulation 954/79[7] was adopted to enable the ratification of the UN Liner

---

[4] *Expanding Horizons – Civil Aviation in Europe, an Action Programme for the Future* (1994).
[5] COM (94) 218 final, *The Way Forward – Civil Aviation in Europe.*
[6] COM (96) 514 final.
[7] OJ 1979 L 121/1.

Conference Code to be compatible with Community law, while Regulation 4055/86[8] applies the principle of freedom to provide services to maritime transport between member states and between member states and third countries. Another measure, Regulation 4058/86,[9] lays down rules on coordinated action to safeguard free access to cargoes in ocean trade. Although this measure does not directly concern access to the Community market, it is included in this chapter owing to its relevance to the Community's maritime industry as a whole. Community shipowners have a significant presence in the highly competitive international maritime services market.

Background
It was not until the end of 1986 that the Community adopted some effective measures. The 1986 maritime package focuses on the threat to Community shipping from the protectionist policies and practices of non-Community countries. Free and non-discriminatory access to cargoes for Community shipowners and fair competition on a commercial basis in trade to, from and within the Community were the overriding principles. The package consisted of four regulations, one of which is aimed at progressively abolishing existing restrictions on the freedom to provide services between member states themselves and between member states and third countries, and to prevent new restrictions being introduced. The other Regulations concern access to cargoes in ocean trade (Regulation 4058/86), the implementation of the EC competition rules to maritime transport (Regulation 4056/86) and unfair pricing practices of non-Community countries (Regulation 4057/86).[10]

UN Liner Conference Code (Regulation 954/79)
The Regulation provides for a definition of 'national shipping lines' which complies with the rules of the EC Treaty on establishment. Member states cannot discriminate between different vessels operating shipping lines established on their territory in accordance with the EC Treaty. In addition, the measure provides for a redistribution, on a commercial basis, of the volume of cargo to which all the shipping lines of the member states participating in the trade are entitled under the Code, irrespective of whether they have the status of 'national shipping line' as defined by the Code. Finally, the Regulation prohibits the application of certain provi-

[8] OJ 1986 L 378/1.
[9] OJ 1986 L 378/21.
[10] OJ 1986 L 378/4 and L 378/14.

sions of the Code (such as the 40:40:20 trade-sharing rule in conference trade) between member states.

Access to international maritime services (Regulation 4055/86)
The Regulation was adopted to assist Community shipowners in fighting restrictions imposed by non-Community countries. The Regulation applies to the carriage of passengers and goods between the ports or off-shore installations of member states and between ports and off-shore installations of a member state and those of a non-Community country, but it does not apply to coastal shipping within a member state, i.e. cabotage.

The Regulation applies: to Community nationals who are established in a member state who provide maritime transport services to others in another member state (Art. 1(1)); to Community nationals who are established outside the Community who provide such services to others in a member state (Art. 1(2)); and to shipping undertakings who are established outside the Community but are 'controlled by nationals of a member state' on condition that the ship is registered 'in that member state in accordance with its legislation' (Art. 1(2)). The Regulation also provides for extension of its scope to nationals of third countries established in the Community if the Council so decides (Art. 7).

Several points should be noted about the scope of this measure. First, it applies to Community nationals established outside the Community but providing services either between member states or between member states and third countries. Secondly, in so far as it covers shipping undertakings controlled by Community nationals, the condition in respect of registration of the ship is not very clear. According to the penultimate recital, this Article was introduced to take account of the structure of the Community shipping industry. The nationals controlling a shipping undertaking appear to have to be nationals of the member state in which the ship is registered. Thus it is not clear, for example, whether a shipping company established in Switzerland, controlled by UK and Dutch nationals and with ships registered in the UK, would be covered by Art. 1. The wording of Art. 1(2) seems to cover just the situation where the control of a shipping undertaking established outside the Community is in the hands of nationals of only one member state. It is submitted, however, that since the Community should be regarded as a whole, the Regulation applies in this case as long as the ship is registered in the UK or in The Netherlands, that is, in one of the member states whose nationality the controllers have. However, it is unlikely that the wording of Art. 1(2) would be interpreted more widely to cover a situation where the ship was not registered in the UK or in The Netherlands but in Spain. There is no definition of 'control' for the purposes of the Regulation. Under Art. 1(3) it is expressly provided that Arts

45 to 48 (ex-Arts 55 to 58) of the EC Treaty apply to matters covered by the Regulation.

The Regulation is concerned with unilateral national restrictions (Art. 2) and bilateral cargo-sharing arrangements concluded with non-Community countries (Art. 3).

As far as unilateral restrictions are concerned, the Regulation applies to existing restrictions but only in respect of the carriage of goods, not passengers. Thus restrictions on the carriage of passengers were prohibited as from the time the Regulation came into force. The Regulation provides a timetable for the gradual phasing-out of these restrictions culminating with their removal from January 1993.

As far as bilateral cargo-sharing arrangements are concerned, restrictions are also to be phased out in accordance with Community law, particularly having regard to the Code of Conduct for Liner Conferences and the Community legislation determining how the 40:40:20 cargo-sharing rule applies to the member states (see above). National shipping lines of one member state are to be treated as if they are national shipping lines of another member state. As to the percentage, Community legislation provides that cargo shares accruing to the national shipping lines of a member state are available for redistribution amongst all members of the conference that are 'national' shipping lines of member states.[11] Favourable arrangements have also been devised, on a reciprocal basis, for shipping lines of OECD countries. As far as trade between member states or on a reciprocal basis between such states and OECD countries which are parties to the Liner Conference Code is concerned, Community legislation[12] provides for the disapplication of the provisions of the Code.

Future cargo-sharing arrangements with non-Community countries are prohibited unless exceptional circumstances arise (Art. 5). These arise where Community shipping undertakings would have no effective opportunity to engage in trade to and from the non-Community country concerned unless such an agreement was entered into. In that case, a specific procedure for approval is to be followed.

Monitoring procedures are also introduced by this measure in respect of the adjustment of existing cargo-sharing arrangements. First, where a member state takes action to adjust an existing arrangement, it must notify

---

[11] A draft Directive on the meaning of 'national shipping line' was part of the 1986 Commission proposals but not adopted. Similarly, a proposal for a regulation (OJ C 263/16) on a common definition of a Community shipowner was published in 1989 but withdrawn in 1996.

[12] See n. 7 above, Art. 4(4).

the other member states and the Commission and then consult the Council. In consulting the Council, the procedure to follow is the one described by Council Decision 77/587[13] setting up a consultation procedure for relations between member states and non-Community countries in shipping matters. Secondly, member states will have to report regularly to the Commission on the progress made in adjusting cargo restrictions in trades not covered by the Code of Conduct. Thirdly, when a problem arises in this area the member state concerned is obliged to inform both the Council and the Commission. If the arrangement is incompatible with the Regulation and the member state concerned so requests, the Council, on a proposal from the Commission, is empowered to take 'appropriate action'.

A procedure is also provided for future cargo-sharing arrangements which might arise owing to 'exceptional circumstances' (Art. 6). First, the member state must inform the other member states and the Commission. Secondly, the Commission will make a proposal to the Council, which, by qualified majority, will take the necessary action, which may include the negotiation and conclusion of a cargo-sharing arrangement. Where the Council does not take a decision within six months, the member state itself may take action. However, the action must be notified to the member states and to the Commission. Consultation as provided by Council Decision 77/587, referred to above, will follow. Any action taken by the member state must be in accordance with Community law and, in particular, provide 'fair, free and non-discriminatory access' to the relevant cargo shares by Community nationals or Community shipping undertakings as defined in Art. 1(1) and (2) of the Regulation. Where a non-Community country tries to impose cargo-sharing arrangements on member states in liquid and dry bulk trades, the Council is empowered under Art. 5(2) to take appropriate action in accordance with the provisions of Regulation 4058/86, which is specifically designed to deal with this particular problem.

It did not take very long for the Regulation to come under the scrutiny of the ECJ. The situation concerned Italy, which signed a cargo-sharing agreement with Algeria three months after the adoption of the Regulation. The Italian government, pursuant to the Regulation, duly informed the Commission. The Commission took the information as initiating a procedure under Art. 6 and submitted a proposal to the Council for a decision authorizing Italy to ratify the agreement subject to the condition that Italy was to modify certain provisions in accordance with Regulation 4055/86

---

13 OJ 1977 L 239/23.

and to take steps to ratify the UN Code of Conduct. This would mean that any cargo-sharing clauses with Algeria would cease to have effect by a given date. The Council, however, allowed Italy to ratify the agreement 'on the understanding' that Italy would ratify the Code.[14] The Commission challenged the Council before the ECJ. Meanwhile, Italy took steps to ratify the code. The ECJ ruled in favour of the Council, stating that the Council was justified by the exceptional circumstances and it had not departed from the objective of the Commission's proposal and had not altered its objective, which was to ensure that the agreement was applied in conformity with Community law.[15]

Free access to cargoes in ocean trades (Regulation 4058/86)
The Regulation applies to practices of non-Community countries and not to practices of shipping undertakings. This is a defensive measure against the practice of non-Community countries restricting access to bulk cargoes, which threatened the application of the principle of fair and free competition in the shipping trade. The relationship between this Regulation and Regulation 4055/86 is not clear but they are closely linked and share the same legal basis and the same goals. The aim of the Regulation is to safeguard the interests of the member states by specifically coordinating action to safeguard free access to cargoes in ocean trades.

A procedure is set up under Arts 3 to 7 to be applied when action by non-Community countries or by their agents, such as freight booking offices, restricts or threatens to restrict free access to cargoes by member states' shipping undertakings or by ships registered in a member state. It should be noted first that the Regulation permits action to be taken against a non-Community country before the restriction arises. If, for example, a non-Community country proposes to enact a national law which will restrict access to member states' shipping undertakings, the Community will be able to take joint action immediately. Secondly, although Art. 1 refers only to member states' shipping undertakings and to ships sailing under the flag of one of the member states, Art. 8 provides for joint action to be taken on behalf of OECD shipping undertakings where, on the basis of reciprocity, there is an agreement between an OECD country and the Community for such action. Thirdly, the cargoes to which the Regulation applies include, according to Art. 1: liner cargoes in non-Code trades and in Code trades except where the non-Community country's action has been

---

14 Decision 87/475, OJ 1987 L 272/37.
15 Case 355/87 *Commission v Council* [1989] ECR 1517.

in accordance with the Code; bulk cargoes and any other cargo on tramp services; passengers; and persons or goods carried to or between off-shore installations. Thus the provisions of the Code of Conduct on a certain amount of cargo-sharing, aimed at helping developing countries, are accepted in traffic between parties who have ratified the Code.

The obligations of the Community and its member states under international law, such as under the Lomé Convention, are also expressly preserved (Art. 1).

Although the coordinated action may be requested by a member state, it must be requested of the Commission and not directly of the Council. It is the Commission, as the initiator of Community action, which has the duty, within four weeks of the request, to make appropriate recommendations or proposals to the Council (Art. 3). The scope of the Commission's recommendations or proposals is outlined in Art. 4. The Commission may propose merely diplomatic representation: this would be appropriate where the non-Community country threatens to restrict access to trade but has not yet taken the final step. However, where the non-Community country has taken action to restrict access, the Commission may propose to the Council that counter-measures be taken directly against the shipping undertakings of the non-Community country concerned or of other non-Community countries which benefit from the action to restrict access. It is irrelevant whether the shipping undertaking benefiting from such action is a home-trader or a cross-trader in Community trade. A home-trader is defined as a shipping undertaking of a non-Community country which operates a service between its own country and one or more member states (as, for example, a Korean ship operating between Korea and France) (Art. 2) while a cross-trader refers to a shipping undertaking of a non-Community country operating a service between another non-Community country and one or more member states (for example, a Korean ship undertaking operating between Australia and France).

The counter-measures proposed by the Commission may take the form of permits, quotas, taxes, duties or a combination of these. However, before such counter-measures are taken, diplomatic representations have to be made. The Council has also to take due account of the Community's external trade policy, the shipping policy of the member state concerned, Community and member states' obligations under international law, port interests and all the interests concerned, and it must ensure that the action taken will not directly or indirectly lead to a deflection of trade within the Community.

Once the matters have been considered, the Council may decide on the appropriate action (Art. 3, para. 3). Whilst a counter-measure applies, member states and the Commission are to consult each other every three months, as provided for by the consultation procedure established by

Council Decision 77/587. This ensures that the effect of the counter-measures are kept under review.

The regulation requires the Council, when deciding whether to take one or more of the counter-measures listed above, to specify certain matters which are listed under Art. 5 as follows:

(a) the developments which have caused counter-measures to be taken;
(b) the trade or range of ports to which counter-measures are to apply;
(c) the flag or shipping undertaking of the non-Community country where cargo reservation measures restrict free access to cargoes in the shipping are concerned;
(d) maximum volume (percentage, weight in tonnes, containers) or value of cargo which may be loaded or discharged in ports of member states;
(e) maximum number of sailings from and to ports of member states;
(f amount or percentage and basis of the taxes and duties to be levied and the manner in which they will be collected; and
(g) the duration of the counter-measures.

Article 5 further provides that where measures such as the imposition of a levy, cannot be taken or implemented under the member states' national legislation, they can be taken by the member states once the Council has issued the enabling decision under Art. 3 of the Regulation. This is an interesting and novel provision, enabling member states whose legislation contains no provision on counter-measures to impose them without having to enact them through the national legislative process. This is possible here only because a regulation is directly applicable, therefore part of national law, and the counter-measures themselves are expressly listed in Art. 4 of the Regulation.

Where the Council fails to adopt the Commission's proposal within a period of two months, the member states may take action unilaterally or as a group (Art. 6). In cases of 'urgency' (which is not defined in the Regulation), member states may take action on a provisional basis, even within the two-month period. In both cases the national measures must be notified to the Commission and to the other member states immediately. The disadvantage of unilateral action is that the interests of the shipping undertakings in some member states are not considered.

The Regulation has been invoked by the Danish government in the context of African freight booking offices, which were alleged to have restricted access by Danish shipping undertakings to West African markets. The Commission proposed to the Council that the first stage of coordinated action, namely diplomatic representations in accordance with Art. 4(2) of the Regulation, should take place. The Council acted upon the Commission's proposal within the framework of the Lomé Convention.

Air transport

Current status

Full market access for Community air carriers to intra-Community air services was granted from April 1997 by Regulation 2408/92, which replaced earlier legislation.[16] Regulation 95/93[17] has also facilitated market access by establishing common rules for the allocation of airport slots.

Background

Scheduled inter-regional air services were the first type of air services to be liberalized. The opening-up of the market was initiated with Directive 83/416,[18] which provided an alternative procedure to that of obtaining traffic rights under bilateral agreements between member states. The Directive, as amended in 1989,[19] applied only to inter-regional air services within the Community operated over 400 km, by aircraft which had a capacity of not more than 70 passenger seats and between two Community airports which were open to international scheduled air traffic. One of the main obstacles to the opening up of the inter-regional services market was the refusal of Spain to include Gibraltar airport in these arrangements. The 1987 civil aviation package was adopted only after a compromise had been reached between Spain and the UK whereby Gibraltar airport was opened up to joint use. The Directive itself was replaced by Regulation 2343/90, which permitted third- and fourth-freedom rights in certain circumstances.[20]

As far as fifth-freedom rights are concerned,[21] Council Decision 87/602[22] permitted airlines to exercise these rights under specified conditions which included authorization of the state of registration. The Irish airline, Aer Lingus, was one of the first airlines to take advantage of the

---

[16] OJ 1992 L 240/8. The Regulation replaced Regulation 2343/90, OJ 1990 L 217/8, on access and on sharing passenger capacity (except for Art. 2(e)(ii) and Annex I) and Regulation 294/91, OJ 1991 L 36/1, on the operation of air cargo services between member states (except Art. 2(b) and the Annex). The exceptions relate to the definition of 'Community air carrier' not meeting the Regulation's definition.

[17] OJ 1993 L 14/1. A new draft directive is under preparation.

[18] OJ 1983 L 237/19.

[19] Directive 89/463 OJ 1989 L 226/14.

[20] OJ 1990 L 217/8. The third freedom right grants airlines the privilege to put down passengers, mail and cargo taken on in the territory of the state whose nationality the aircraft possesses. The fourth freedom grants the right to take on passengers, mail and cargo destined for the territory of the state whose nationality the aircraft possesses.

[21] The right to pick up passengers in a state other than the state of registration and to set down those passengers in a third state.

[22] OJ 1987 L 374/19.

fifth-freedom right granted under the 1987 Decision. On its Dublin-Milan flight Aer Lingus wished to pick up passengers in Manchester. Italy, however, refused to allow this, on the ground that Milan airport qualified for an exemption from opening regional routes to competitors. Decision 87/602 was also replaced by Regulation 2343/90. As far as the allocation of slots is concerned, the major problem for the Community was to reform the system of allocating take-off and landing slots at Community airports which was based on 'historic rights' (also known as 'grandfather rights'). A 'historic right' is the right to a slot in one season because an airline operated the service in that particular slot in the previous year. The Commission was concerned that congestion would impede the liberalization process and, therefore, decided that Community measures were necessary. A Code of Conduct, adopted in 1993, sets out common rules aimed at ensuring neutral, transparent and non-discriminatory decisions on the allocation of slots at congested airports. The Code was followed by legislation (i.e. Regulation 95/93).

Right of access (Regulation 2408/92)

The holding of an operational licence does not necessarily grant the holder rights of access to specific routes.[23] Since the abolition of bilateral agreements between member states regulating access rights, a Community undertaking, irrespective of nationality, may operate as an air carrier anywhere in the Community whenever opportunities might exist. Thus the Regulation seeks to ensure that Community air carriers have freedom to provide services in intra-Community air routes including cabotage (Art. 3(1) and (2)).

The distinction between scheduled and non-scheduled air services which had had a significant role in the liberalization of air transport services has been eliminated (Art. 1(1)). The operator now has complete freedom on how to provide the services.

The Regulation, however, does provide for the possibility of safeguard measures being adopted which may restrict the market access freedom. These safeguard measures may be adopted to pursue national policy objectives such as the maintenance of scheduled services which are in the public interest (Art. 4(1)(a)) or the reduction of airport congestion or the protection of the environment (Art. 9). However, the Community institutions have been given special enforcement powers in order to be able to scruti-

---

23 See Regulation 2407/92, OJ 1992 L 240/1, below.

nize any national measures adopted under these safeguard clauses.[24] Soon after the adoption of the Regulation, the Commission was given the opportunity to interpret Arts 3(1) and 8(1). France refused to permit Viva Air to operate scheduled services between Madrid and Paris (De Gaulle airport) on grounds that Iberia, a member of the same group, already flew Madrid-Paris (Orly airport). The Commission considered that the refusal did not conform with the Regulation.[25] The Commission decided that Art. 8(1), permitting a restriction on the general principle of freedom of access granted in Art. 3(1), was to be interpreted strictly, like any exception to a general principle. Furthermore, any application of that restriction must be based on transparent and objective criteria, which must remain constant over a given period and be non-discriminatory.

Access to some airports continues to cause controversy.[26] In addition, lack of airport slots, infrastructure limitations and environmental considerations have also an impact on the exercise of the freedom.

Allocation of airport slots (Regulation 95/93)

In the air transport sector the allocation of airport slots causes similar problems as quotas in road transport. Thus the Community has had to adopt specific legislation on the allocation of airport slots. It imposes on member states responsibility for deciding on the need for slot allocation through a capacity analysis, for designating a congested airport as a coordinated or fully coordinated airport and for appointing a coordinator who shall carry out the duties in an independent manner.

The Regulation is based on existing IATA practice but is aimed to make the system work more fairly, more uniformly and more efficiently. The Regulation seeks to protect the legitimate interests of established carriers (i.e. 'grandfather rights') but also to promote competition by assisting new entrants (Art. 8). The Regulation includes stricter rules relating to non-use of slots than those in the IATA guidelines (the 'use it or lose it' rule). Airlines not using 80% of a series of slots without good reason stand to lose the whole series (Art. 10(5)). Dispensation is provided for charter carriers affected by cancellations by tour operators. In reality, however, the Regulation has not led to an increase in airline competition; only a small

---

[24] See for example in respect of public service obligations: OJ 1997 C 154/3 and C 243/2 (France) and C 312/15 (Ireland).

[25] Commission Decision 93/347, OJ 1993 L 140/51.

[26] See, for example, Commission Decisions 94/290, OJ 1994 L 127/22 and 95/259, OJ 1995 L 162/25 concerning the French/British disagreement over access to Orly airport in France.

percentage of the slots allocated to new entrants are during the times when most passengers wish to fly.

The Regulation lists conditions for designation of coordinated airports, including initial and subsequent capacity analyses (Art. 3). It provides for the appointment of independent coordinators and their duties (Art. 4). Scheduling committees are to be established with stated responsibilities including dispute-solving procedures (Art. 5). In certain narrowly defined circumstances, slots for domestic services are protected (Art. 9). A safeguard mechanism to replace the 'reciprocity' provision in the second and third packages is provided but also in narrowly defined circumstances (Art. 11).

Tariffs

Maritime

Council Regulation 4056/86[27] was adopted applying the competition rules, Arts 81 and 82 of the EC Treaty, to maritime transport. Thus price-fixing agreements between maritime undertakings became subject to the strict competition rules except for certain types of agreements expressly exempted under the Regulation.

Air transport

Current status
Fares and rates for air transport services are governed by Regulation 2409/92[28] and the EC competition rules.

Background
The Chicago Convention expressly left the negotiations of tariffs to the airlines, usually with reference to the tariff agreements concluded under the auspices of the International Air Transport Association. The tariff agreements are subject to the approval of the governments of both contracting states. One of the main benefits of this system has been the operation of 'interlining', which enables air tickets paid in the currency of a contracting state to be accepted by most airlines of the world.

Since the 1984 Commission Memorandum, changes have been aimed at improving airline services and decreasing fares. In *Nouvelles Frontieres*[29] the ECJ concluded that Art. 11 of the EC Treaty in conjunction with Art. 3(f) and Art. 81 made it unlawful for member states to approve air tariffs

---

[27] OJ 1986 L 378/4.
[28] OJ 1992 L 240/15.
[29] See n. 2 above.

which have been concluded as a result of agreements or concerted practices between airlines. Airlines must fix fares unilaterally in accordance with market conditions, and exemptions from the EC competition rules should be granted for certain agreements.

The 1987 civil aviation package included Directive 87/601[30] on the fixing of air fares for scheduled flights within the Community. This Directive was replaced by Regulation 2342/90,[31] which provided criteria and procedures for establishing tariffs on scheduled air services on routes between Community airports. The Regulation in turn was replaced by Regulation 2409/92.

Air fares (Regulation 2409/92)
The Regulation establishes the principle that air carriers are free to set fares for the services they operate within the Community (Art. 5(1)). The same principles apply to charter fares to be paid by the passengers on non-scheduled flights, and to cargo rates (Art. 3).[32]

Air fares are therefore no longer subject to prior approval of member states although the Regulation provides for the possibility of member states requiring the filing of such fares at least 24 hours before they become effective (Art. 5(2)).

Two safeguard clauses are contained in the Regulation enabling member states, under specified conditions, either to withdraw excessively high basic fares or to stop further fare decreases in case of substantial downward development of air fares which has led to significant losses being incurred by all carriers operating the route (Art. 6(1)).

The Commission is empowered to examine, at the request of a member state or on the basis of a complaint, the legality of any action taken by the competent national authorities under Art. 6.

Rights of non-resident undertakings

Maritime transport

Current status
Regulation 3577/92[33] was adopted applying the principle of freedom to

---

[30] OJ 1987 L 374/12.
[31] OJ 1990 L 217/1.
[32] The Regulation does not apply to fares and rates established by public service obligations in accordance with Regulation 2408/92 on access to Community air routes (Art. 1(2)(b)).
[33] OJ 1992 L 364/7.

provide services to maritime transport within member states from 1 January 1993.

Background

Regulation 4055/86 on access to maritime transport services did not introduce cabotage, although a proposal to that effect had been on the table. Some member states, such as the UK, Ireland, Denmark and the Netherlands, traditionally follow an open coastline policy, while others, such as Italy, Greece, France and Spain, restricted mainland cargo cabotage and inland passenger operations to ships carrying their national flags. However, it was agreed that further consideration should be given to the proposal and such a proposal was tabled with the 1989 maritime package proposals.

Maritime cabotage (Regulation 3577/92)

The Regulation allows cabotage trade from 1993 onwards for Community shipowners which have their ships registered in, and flying the flag of, a member state, provided the vessels comply with all the conditions for carrying out cabotage in that member state (Art. 1(1)). Community shipowners are defined in the same manner as for Regulation 4055/86 discussed above (Art. 2(2)).

The Regulation covers mainland cabotage, off-shore supply services and island cabotage (Art. 2(1)). Many concessions were granted but the only remaining derogation relates to Greece, where a derogation was granted until 2004 for regular passenger vessels, ferry services and services provided by vessels less than 650 gross registered tonnage ('grt'). Only after 1999 did the laws of the state of registration of the ship (the flag state) apply to the crew operating ships over 650 grt. Until then the host state's legislation applied. For ships under 650 grt the host state's laws will apply indefinitely.

The Regulation establishes the manning conditions applicable in the different trades. The home state (the flag state) conditions apply to mainland cabotage and to cruise services except for ships smaller than 650 grt (Art. 3(1)). From January 1999, the home state's laws also apply to the manning of cargo vessels over 650 grt engaged in so-called consecutive island cabotage (the island cabotage voyage concerned follows or precedes a voyage to or from another member state) (Art. 3(3)).

However, for all cabotage services with ships below 650 grt and all other types of island cabotage, the Regulation provides that all matters relating to manning shall be the responsibility of the state in which the vessel performs maritime transport (host state) (Art. 3(2)).

The measure also contains a safeguard clause in the event of serious disturbance of the internal transport market due to cabotage liberalization. At the request of a member state the Commission may adopt safeguard measures which may involve a temporary exclusion not exceeding 12 months of the area concerned from the scope of the Regulation. In the event of an emergency member states may unilaterally adopt the appropriate provisional measures which may remain in force for no more than three months. The Commission shall be notified immediately and shall confirm or abrogate the measures, before it takes a final decision (Art. 5).

As long as certain conditions are met, the Regulation permits the member states to conclude public service contracts with, or impose public service obligations as a condition for the provision of cabotage services on, shipping undertakings participating in regular services to, from and between islands (Art. 4).

The Commission adopted a Decision[34] under Art. 5(1) reversing Spain's unilateral action in suspending the operation of cabotage but, a few months later, adopted another Decision[35] granting certain coastal maritime transport services a further six-month transition period before becoming subject to the cabotage Regulation.

A proposal to amend this Regulation is under discussion which will enable host member states to determine the proportion of Community nationals which cruise ships must have when operating in their waters.[36]

Air transport

The 1987 package did not permit cabotage nor were the member states able to agree cabotage rights in the 1990 package. However, Art. 3 of Regulation 2408/92 (the market access regulation) provides for carriers to fly any intra-Community route from 1 April 1997. Community carriers holding Community operating licences granted by their national authorities are able to operate entirely self-contained domestic services within the territory of other member states.

Removal of restrictions on access to the occupation of transport services operator

Maritime transport

It is clear under the general provisions of the EC Treaty in respect of the right of establishment (Arts 43 to 48) that any national laws restricting the

---

[34] Decision 93/125, OJ 1993 L 49/88.
[35] Decision 93/396, OJ 1993 L 173/33.
[36] COM (98) 251.

right of establishment of shipping companies from one member state to another are unenforceable as against EC natural and legal persons. Regulation 613/91[37] facilitates the transfer of ships from one register to another within the Community.

Registration of ships

A matter closely related to the right of establishment is registration under the national flag. Does a shipping company incorporated in one member state and having the right of establishment in another, also obtain, by the exercise of that right, the right to register its ship under the national flag? On the one hand the Commission considers that registration is a corollary of establishment, while member states hold the view that permitting registration under their flags is akin to the granting of nationality to a person, that is, an exercise of sovereignty. The effect of the EC Treaty right of establishment provisions on the sovereign right of the member states to determine the conditions for registration in their national ship registers has been the subject of a ruling from the ECJ in *Factortame II*.[38]

The Court ruled that:

> As Community law stands at present, it is for the member states to determine, in accordance with the general rules of international law, the conditions which must be fulfilled in order for a vessel to be registered in their registers and granted the right to fly their flag. In exercising that power, the member states must nevertheless comply with the rules of Community law.

In *Factortame* the Court found that it was contrary to Community law for the UK to require that the owners, charterers, managers and operators of the vessels in the UK Register be nationals of that member state, or companies incorporated therein where ownership and management is at least 75% by UK nationals. However, the ECJ concluded that it is not contrary to Community law for a member state to stipulate as a condition for vessel registration in the national register that the vessel must be managed and its operations directed and controlled from within that member state.

Furthermore, it was explicitly recognized that once an undertaking fulfils the establishment criteria of a given member state and becomes an undertaking in that state, it has the right under the EC Treaty to establish in any other member state and thus have access to that member state's ship register.[39] The ECJ has also taken the opportunity to explore the general French

---

[37] OJ 1991 L 68/1, subsequently amended to incorporate upgraded international standards.
[38] Case C-221/89, *R v Secretary of State for Transport, ex p Factortame* [1991] ECR 3905.
[39] See Case C-62/96 *Commission v Greece* [1997] ECR I-6725.

regime on the registration of ships and their right to the French flag. The opportunity arose by the failure of France to comply with a 1974 judgment, the *Code Maritime Case*.[40] Twenty years after the judgment the Commission decided to initiate an infringement procedure under Art. 226 against France for this 'surprisingly long' failure.[41] French law contained strict rules, contrary to Community law, in respect of the ownership of ships that could be registered in France.

The Commission has abandoned the idea of introducing a Community ship register (EUROS) which it had proposed in the 1989 maritime package. Instead, it proposes to ensure that all the registers of the member states meet certain criteria concerning obligations imposed on shipowners and their enforcement.

Ship register transfers (Regulation 613/91)

The Regulation's objective is to permit the transfer of ships from one register to another within the Community by preventing member states withholding from registration ships registered in other member states which comply with the international requirements and carry valid certificates (Art. 3). The measure applies to cargo ships of 500 grt and upwards which were built after 1980 (or if built earlier comply with the 1974 Safety of Life at Sea Convention (SOLAS)) and which have been flying the flag of, and have been registered in, a member state for at least six months and carry valid certificates (Art. 2).

Refusal to transfer on the grounds of interpretation of requirements or provisions left by Conventions to the discretion of member states have to be notified to the Commission (Art. 5).

Air transport

Airlines operate on the basis of a Community licence. Regulation 2407/92[42] on licensing of air carriers requires the member state granting the licence to take into account the applicant's technical capability and economic and financial viability.

Community operating licence (Regulation 2407/92)

The Regulation establishes common and uniform criteria for the licensing of Community air carriers. No undertaking established in the Community may carry passengers, mail or cargo commercially (even within national

---

[40] Case 167/73 *Commission v France* [1974] ECR 359. See Chapter 2.
[41] Case C-334/94 *Commission v France* [1994] ECR I-1307.
[42] OJ 1992 L 240/1.

territory) unless an appropriate operating licence has been granted (Art. 3(3)).

An air carrier undertaking is entitled to a licence if certain conditions are met. First, the undertaking must have its principal place of business and registered office in the licensing member state. Secondly, the undertaking must be primarily engaged in air transport, either in isolation or combined with any other commercial operation of aircraft or repair and maintenance of aircraft. Thirdly, the undertaking must be owned and effectively controlled by member states or Community nationals. In addition, the undertaking must have a sound financial basis and a management of good reputation (Arts 5(1) and 6(1)). The applicant has to submit a business plan for at least the first two years of operation and any future alterations to that plan (Art. 5(2)). Licensing authorities may at any time assess the licensed air carrier's financial performance and may suspend or revoke the licence (Art. 5(5)). The applicant must be insured to cover liability in case of accidents (Art. 7). Finally, the undertaking must hold a valid air operator's certificate (Art. 9).

If all of the above conditions are met, the applicant is entitled to be licensed as an air carrier. However, such a licence does not confer in itself any right of access to specific routes or markets (Art. 3(2)).

Prior approval of the appropriate licensing authority is required where the licensed air carrier uses aircraft of another undertaking (Art. 8 on leasing arrangements). The Regulation also provides for the undertaking whose application for an operating licence has been refused to refer the dispute to the Commission (Art. 13(3)).

As far as access to the market is concerned, the holder of a Community licence's freedom must not be restricted by conditions attached to the licence which have no foundation in the third civil aviation package of legislative measures. The scope of the licence, for example, must not be limited to specific intra-Community routes or to the provision of either scheduled or non-scheduled services.

The third civil aviation package is based on the principles of mutual recognition of operating licences and home state control. Licences must be recognized by all member states and market access must not be refused on grounds that the licensed carrier does no longer comply with the conditions of Regulation 2407/92. Any verification of such compliance is exclusively a matter for the licensing member state.

Concluding observations

It took a long time for the Community to adopt the necessary legislation to open up the Community market to these two modes of transport. The international nature of these services, together with the direct national interests of the governments of the member states in the operation of these services made it a difficult goal to achieve. The overall political agreement of the member states on establishing an internal market by 1992 gave the Community the impetus to act. However, the tough negotiations at Community level and the heavy lobbying of the industries themselves ensured that the liberalization of the market, in particular the air transport market, was only achieved by stages. Nevertheless, at the beginning of the twenty-first century the necessary measures to open up both markets are in place. Whether a true free internal market for the provision of maritime and air services will be a reality depends now on economic and political factors.

CHAPTER 5

Indirect liberalization: harmonization

Introduction

Liberalization of the transport market requires not only the removal of restrictions on access to that market but also uniform or quasi-uniform operational conditions in national markets. The different national operational rules impose a dual burden on the non-established undertakings if they have to meet the requirements of both the home and host member state. Business is run in accordance with the rules and regulations of the home member state (the state of establishment) and so it would incur extra costs if it also had to meet the host state requirements which might differ slightly or substantially from the home state's. Furthermore, different national rules may deter undertakings from operating in another member state and therefore defeat the goal of market integration. Less strict national rules may also have an effect on competition, since fewer operational costs enable transport providers to offer lower tariffs than competitors from other member states. This not only affects the competitiveness of the transport industry itself but also it has a knock-on effect on the end products.

Community policy, therefore, is to harmonize national measures, stipulating a minimum Community criteria which has to be met. Individual member states may have stricter requirements for undertakings established in their territory but they cannot demand that non-established undertakings meet these stricter requirements. Thus the directive is the legislative measure chosen to ensure basic harmonization; sometimes the Council will adopt a framework directive conferring power on the Commission to adopt implementing measures or to adapt the original directive to advance technical progress.

Social measures: living and working conditions

The original legislation in this area was aimed at ensuring that the different levels of social protection in member states did not distort competition.

Thus the legislation was aimed at harmonizing working conditions in inland transport and conditions as to crews, rest periods, and introducing procedures for checking compliance. Council Decision 65/271[1] provided that, after 1966, each method of transport was to harmonize legislative, regulatory and administrative provisions. This was then to be followed by the harmonization of provisions relating to the working conditions in all three modes of transport, taking into account the differences in techniques and the functions to be fulfilled. Provisions on the composition of crews in each transport mode were to be harmonized by 1967. At the same time, regulations relating to hours worked and rest periods were also to be harmonized. After 1967 provisions relating to overtime and the basis of calculating it were to be determined. This harmonization was to be completed by 1968 at the latest. Finally, after 1967, road transport workers were to be issued with a record book in order to keep track of whether the provisions governing hours worked had been complied with; the same would be done for workers in inland waterway undertakings after 1 July 1967.

In the 1980s the Commission set up Joint Committees for each mode of transport. The first Joint Committee was set up for inland navigation in 1980.[2] Four years later similar committees were set up for railways[3] and for road transport.[4] Joint Committees were set up for maritime transport in 1987 and for civil aviation in 1990.[5] Each Committee, a representative forum for the socio-economic interests involved, consists of members appointed by the Commission on a proposal from the carriers' association and the employees' association. The main objective of these Committees is to ensure that all interested parties for each mode of transport participate and assist the Commission in the formulation and implementation of the Community's social policy and in harmonizing living and working conditions by issuing opinions and submitting reports to the Commission, promoting dialogue and cooperation.

Finally, the 1997 White Paper, *Sectors of Activities Excluded from the Working Time Directive* (Directive 93/104[6]), concluded that the concept of limiting the hours of work must be introduced to the transport industry in

---

1 JO 1965 No. 88, p. 1500.
2 Commission Decision 80/991, OJ 1980 L 297/28.
3 Commission Decision 85/13, OJ 1985 L 8/26, subsequently amended.
4 Commission Decision 85/516, OJ 1985 L 317/33.
5 Commission Decision 87/467, OJ 1987 L 253/30 and Commission Decision 90/449, OJ 1990 L 230/22.
6 OJ 1993 L 307/8.

order to align existing social legislation with that in force for other industries. It is proposed that the Directive will apply to the following: non-mobile workers in all sectors, including road, maritime, air and rail transport; railway workers; and workers on off-shore oil and natural gas platforms. The proposal not only applies the standards of the 1993 Directive to all non-mobile workers but also provides specific rules for road and maritime modes of transport. Derogations will be allowed from some of the provisions of the Directive provided that the workers concerned are afforded equivalent periods of compensatory rest.

Although Regulation 3820/85, discussed below, already provides maximum daily working periods, breaks and daily rest periods, there are, however, important differences between these provisions and those of the Working Time Directive. Regulation 3820/85 seeks to harmonize conditions of competition between all types of road transport operators as well as to impose road safety and working conditions. The Regulation does not stipulate the maximum hours for activities other than driving.

Road transport

Current status

Two main measures govern the Community's social policy in transport. The Community's social legislation is set out in Regulation 3820/85[7] and Regulation 3821/85[8] on recording (tachograph) equipment. The provisions of the tachograph regulation have been strengthened by Regulation 2135/98.[9] Directive 88/599[10] was adopted on the standard checking procedures for the implementation of these Regulations.[11]

Background

In 1993 the Commission set up a 'Wisemen' Committee[12] to investigate the economic and social situation in the road haulage sector. One of the

---

[7] OJ 1985 L 370/1, which replaced Regulation 543/69, OJ 1969 L 77/49, as amended.

[8] OJ 1985 L 370/8 as amended. The Regulation replaced Regulation 1463/70, OJ 1970 L 164/1, which had introduced the tachograph to ensure compliance with drivers' hours. The Regulation has been adapted to technical progress on several occasions by Commission Regulations.

[9] OJ 1998 L 274/1.

[10] OJ 1988 L 325/55, as amended.

[11] Both Regulations have often been subject to interpretation by the ECJ under an Art. 234 preliminary procedure, e.g. Case C-116/91 *Licensing Authority South Eastern Traffic Area v British Gas plc* [1992] ECR I-4071.

[12] A small group of experts called either 'Wisemen' or 'High-Level' which have been set up by the Commission to consider various transport issues and make recommendations.

issues raised in their report[13] was the substantial breaches of operating regulations. The lack of enforcement of regulations was identified as the single greatest problem facing the sector: enforcement in general should be improved and there should be particular emphasis on the enforcement of social legislation. Following the 'Wisemen's' report, the Council adopted Resolutions on Social Harmonization in Road Freight Transport.[14] The Commission was requested to carry out a comparative study of the training of drivers of heavy goods vehicles and of the market conditions and regulations in the different member states, and to examine ways to improve cooperation between governments, particularly to prevent breaches of social provisions. The Commission was requested to assess the effectiveness of the social harmonization regulations and to prepare amendments if required to Directive 88/599 with a view to incorporating best control practices.

Working conditions (Regulation 3820/85)

Regulation 3820/85 concerns such matters as the age of drivers of vehicles not exempted by the measure (Art. 4), driving periods and rest periods. The minimum age of drivers engaged in the carriage of goods or passengers is primarily 21 years. The minimum age of drivers engaged in the carriage of goods in vehicles which are not too heavy is 18 years provided they hold a certificate of professional competence in conformity with Community rules (Art. 5(1)). The minimum age for drivers' mates and conductors is 18 (Art. 5(3)).

The Regulation also states that drivers must meet one of the following conditions. First, they must have worked for at least one year in the carriage of goods as a driver of motor vehicles with a permissible maximum weight exceeding 3.5 tonnes. Secondly, they must have worked for at least one year as a driver of motor vehicles used for the carriage of passengers on regular services where the route covered by the service in question does not exceed a 50 km radius from the place where the vehicle is normally based. Thirdly, they must hold a certificate of professional competence recognized by one of the member states confirming that they have completed a training course for drivers of vehicles intended for the carriage of passengers by road (Art. 5(2)).

---

[13] *The Transport of Goods by Road in the Heart of the Single European Market* (1994). It was also recommended that the Commission should adopt measures to ensure road transport develops in a competitive framework without barriers or distortions. It is necessary to have identical conditions of access to the profession in the single market.

[14] OJ 1994 C 309/4 and OJ 1995 C 169/4.

As far as driving periods are concerned, the Regulation is very specific. For example, no driver may exceed 4½ hours without a break for 45 minutes (Art. 7(1)). As a general rule, the total period of driving between two consecutive daily rest periods ('the daily driving period') is not to exceed 9 hours (Art. 6(1)). Similarly, every driver must have a daily rest period of at least 11 consecutive hours (Art. 8(1)). There are exceptions to all these basic rules but the exceptions themselves are very specific. In addition to daily rest periods, rules are also laid down for weekly rest periods (Art. 6)).

In order to ensure compliance, the Regulation itself prohibits certain incentive payments which may encourage drivers to break the rules. Bonuses or payments related to distance travelled or to the amount of goods carried are prohibited (Art. 10). Member states have an obligation to adopt the necessary national measures to ensure compliance including penalties for breach.[15] Control procedures and penalties are also provided for those vehicles which are not fitted with tachographs in accordance with Council Regulation 3821/85.

There are several derogations to the provisions of the legislation, such as, for example, vehicles used by the police or ambulances. Each member state may also apply higher minimum norms on rest or lower maximum norms on driving periods than those laid down in the Regulation (Art. 11). Every two years the Commission is obliged to produce a report on the implementation of this Regulation (Art. 16).

The tachograph (Regulation 3821/85)

As far as recording equipment (the tachograph) is concerned, Regulation 3821/85 replaced previous measures. The Regulation lays down provisions concerning the construction, installation, use and testing of recording equipment in vehicles used for carriage of goods and passengers. The Regulation provides for member states exemptions (Art. 3) and contains detailed provisions on type approval of the recording equipment (Arts 4 to 11), and installation and inspection and use of equipment (Arts 12 to 16). The Annexes provide the technical details. The tachograph itself is subject to EC approval, and a model record sheet has been devised. Any vehicle fitted with an approved tachograph cannot be refused registration by a member state. Such tachographs can be installed only by workshops approved by competent national authorities. The employer and crew mem-

---

[15] In Case 326/88 *Ministère Public v Hansen & Son* [1990] ECR I-2911, the ECJ ruled that nothing in EC legislation prevented a member state from imposing penal liability 'without fault' on the employer of a lorry driver who violated EC regulations in respect of working hours.

bers are responsible for ensuring that the tachograph functions correctly (Art. 13). The record sheets must be retained by the employer for at least one year and the sheets are to be produced or handed over at the request of any authorized inspecting officer (Art. 14(2)).

As there was evidence that the rules were being infringed, Regulation 2135/98 was adopted with the objective of improving the enforcement and compliance of the tachograph Regulation. The Regulation provides for compulsory installation of fully digital recording equipment on all new vehicles as from the end of 2000 if all the conditions laid down are satisfied. The new recording equipment records all the activities of the driver on board the vehicle and stores them for one year. The vehicle must be equipped with a printer. Each driver must have his own microprocessor card within which all his activities are recorded.

Railways

As railway workers were considered to be relatively well protected at national level by collective agreements, Council Decision 65/271[16] did not apply to railways. Thus living and working conditions of railway workers are governed by national law. However, it is intended to extend the Working Time Directive to all workers. This will have a significant impact on long distance train drivers and appropriate adjustments are being negotiated.

Inland waterways

Not much has been adopted concerning the working conditions in this sector. However, Art. 8 of Regulation 718/99,[17] which lays down a Community-fleet capacity policy to promote this mode of transport, provides an example of some legislative action. Member states are permitted to take supporting measures to make it easier for carriers leaving the industry such as offering an early retirement pension or a transfer to another economic activity. Early retirement pensions may be granted to workers leaving the inland waterways industry as a result of scrapping schemes. National measures may also be adopted to organize vocational training courses or retraining courses.

Maritime transport

Current status and background

As far as the maritime sector is concerned, a few measures have been adopted concerning the health of sailors and their working conditions.

---

[16] JO 1965 No. 88, p. 1500.
[17] OJ 1999 L 90/1. See also Chapter 3.

Traditionally, such matters are governed by the state where the vessel is registered ('the flag state'). The Community, however, recognizes that the health of workers on board a vessel, which is a high-risk workplace, requires special attention. As far as living and working conditions are concerned, Directive 92/29[18] on medical treatment aboard vessels and Directive 99/95[19] on working time for seafarers on board ships calling at Community ports are the only specific measures adopted in this area. Directive 95/21 ('the Port State Control Directive')[20] provides, *inter alia*, for a right to act where the conditions on board do not meet international rules on living and working conditions on board.

A proposal for a directive on working conditions of seafarers on scheduled passenger and ferry services operating between ports in the Community is under discussion.[21] The proposed directive will apply to non-Community seafarers in order to prevent social dumping.

Medical treatment on board (Directive 92/29)

Minimum safety and health requirements for improved medical treatment on board vessels registered in the Community are set out in this Directive. The measure seeks to ensure that adequate medical supplies are available so that workers can obtain the necessary medical treatment at sea.

The Directive imposes an obligation on the member states to ensure that shipowners comply with the minimum requirements. In addition to the requirement of adequate medical supplies (Art. 2(1)), the Directive also requires vessels of more than 500 grt with a crew of 15 or more workers to have a sick-bay (Art. 2(3)) and for vessels with a crew of 100 or more workers engaged on an international voyage of more than three days to have a doctor on board (Art. 2(4)). The Directive also envisages medical consultation by radio or satellite (Art. 6). Specific provision is made in the Directive for antidotes to be available on board when dangerous substances are being carried (Art. 3).

Finally, member states are required to ensure that the responsibility for complying with the provisions lies with the shipowners (Art. 4), that special training has been received by those using medical supplies (Art. 5) and that annual inspections of vessels are undertaken to check compliance (Art. 7).

---

[18] OJ 1992 L 113/19.
[19] OJ 1991 L 14/29.
[20] OJ 1995 L 157/1, subsequently amended.
[21] COM (98) 251 final.

Working time for seafarers (Directive 99/95)

This measure concerns the working periods of crew on board vessels calling at Community ports. Its purpose is to apply the provisions of Directive 99/63[22] which incorporates into Community law an Agreement on working time concluded between shipowners and trade unions (Art. 1). The Agreement reflects the provisions of the International Labour Organisation (ILO) Convention 180 on working time. Directive 99/95 goes beyond the ILO provisions as it applies to vessels flying a non-Community flag but operating in European Community waters (Art. 9). The measure seeks to combat unfair competition due to social dumping. Community seafarers are increasingly being replaced by non-Community workers who have less social protection.

Port state control (Directive 95/21)

Among its objectives Directive 95/21 lists compliance with international and relevant Community legislation on living and working conditions on board. The Directive applies to ships of all flags (Art. 1). The Directive applies to all merchant shipping and crews using a seaport of a member state or off-shore terminal or anchored off such port or installation (Art. 3).

Air transport

Although the European Parliament has called for the harmonization of social conditions that will guarantee high social protection levels for workers in the industry, the Commission has so far introduced very limited proposals. The Commission's proposals provide for the application of the Working Time Directive[23] to the aviation sector but only for non-mobile workers such as airport and airline ground staff. Specific measures will be adopted for mobile workers through the ongoing work on a uniform regulatory system for flight time limitations. This work is being undertaken by the Commission and the Joint Air Authorities (JAA).

Safety and environment protection

Safety is a key feature of all modes of transport and is not confined to transport in the Community. Many international Conventions have been negotiated and signed imposing responsibility on states to ensure that their national transport industries meet minimum agreed standards. Specific leg-

---

[22] OJ 1999 L 167/33.
[23] See n. 6 above.

islation, considered below, has been adopted in respect of the carriage of dangerous goods. In addition, Directive 96/35[24] harmonizes the appointment and vocational qualifications of safety advisers for the transport of dangerous goods by road, rail and inland waterways. A proposal for a directive on the harmonization of the examination requirements for safety advisers is under consideration.[25]

The significance of the environment in the context of transport policy is a more recent development but has been recognized at the highest levels, including the Community institutions. In June 1998, for the first time, a joint meeting of the Transport and Environment Councils took place. This signalled a cultural change and a recognition that the protection of the environment is a significant feature of transport policy.

Safety advisers (Directive 96/35)

Directive 96/35 imposed a duty on member states to ensure, by 31 December 1999, that each undertaking involved in the carriage of dangerous goods appoints one or more safety advisers responsible for helping to prevent risks inherent in such activities as far as persons, property and the environment are concerned (Art. 1). The main task of the adviser is to seek all appropriate means and take appropriate action to facilitate the conduct of the undertaking's activities in accordance with the law in the safest possible way (Art. 4(1)). The adviser does not have to be independent of the undertaking. The adviser may be directly employed by the undertaking, or even its head, as long as it is demonstrated that the person is capable of performing the duties of adviser (Art. 4(2)). The adviser has to hold a Community-type vocational training certificate, which requires training and passing an examination on subjects listed in an Annex and approved by the national competent authorities (Art. 5). The certificate is valid for five years (Art. 6). In discharging his responsibility the adviser must prepare a report on any accident which affected a person, property or the environment (Art. 7).

Road transport

The 1997 Commission Communication setting out an Action Plan for 1997–2001, adopted a new approach to road transport safety concentrating on the following themes: information so as to ensure that the collection and diffusion of information and 'best practice' is set up for an integrated

---

[24] OJ 1996 L 145/10.
[25] COM (2000) 112 final.

EC information system; prevention, meaning initiating and promoting measures intended to prevent accidents; and reduction of the consequences of accidents.

Information: accident statistics and programmes

A Community-wide database called CARE was established to provide detailed information on road accidents.[26] The absence of a common database was hampering analyses of road safety problems. The member states are required to establish statistics on road accidents resulting in death or injury that occur in their territories (Art. 1). The information has to be sent to the Community's Statistical Office (Art. 2). The database will facilitate in-depth analysis of road safety and provide the basis for further joint action in this area.

Directive 72/166[27] harmonizes national laws in respect of insurance and civil liability of vehicles' owners. The Directive safeguards the victims of accidents by means of a network of agreements between national insurers' bureaux of the member states. Each national bureau guarantees compensation in accordance with the provisions of national laws on compulsory insurance in respect of claims arising out of accidents caused in its territory by a vehicle normally based in another member state.

Several studies have been financed with EUREKA, a research and development programme. In 1988 the Council adopted a specific Community programme in the field of road transport informatics and telecommunications, worth EUR 60 million.[28] The programme has a number of objectives including promoting road safety.

Prevention: training, driving licences and speed limits

As far as training is concerned, several measures have been adopted. Directive 76/914[29] lays down the minimum level of training required for drivers of passenger and goods vehicles to satisfy the condition of professional competence.[30] The Directive provides that only persons possessing the appropriate national driving licence and who have completed a course of vocational training covering at least the subjects specified in the Directive are to be recognized as having the minimum level of training for

---

[26] Decision 93/704, OJ 1993 L 329/63.
[27] OJ 1972 L 103/1.
[28] Decision 88/416, OJ 1988 L 206/1 setting up: Dedicated Road Information for Vehicle Safety in Europe (DRIVE).
[29] OJ 1976 L 357/36.
[30] Directives 89/48, OJ 1989 L 19/16 and 92/51, OJ 1992 L 209/25.

drivers of vehicles intended for the carriage of goods or passengers by road (Art. 1).

A certificate of professional competence has to be issued by national competent authorities where the person concerned meets the requirements laid down in the Directive (Art. 2(1)).

As far as the carriage of dangerous goods by road is concerned, vocational training for drivers is governed by Directive 94/55.[31] The Directive implements throughout the Community the requirements of the 1957 (as amended) Agreement on the International Carriage of Dangerous Goods by Road (ADR). The drivers of these vehicles must hold a vocational training certificate, valid for up to five years, confirming they have successfully completed appropriate training. Vehicles belonging to a member state's armed forces do not come within the scope of this measure (Art. 1(1)). A standardized training programme is set out ensuring that drivers are aware of the risks and imparting basic knowledge to minimize the chance of an accident occurring (Art. 4). More extensive training may be required by member states for drivers of vehicles registered in that member state (Art. 4(3)).

As far as driving licences are concerned, Community legislation has existed since 1980, when national driving licences were required to be issued in accordance with the Community model set out in an Annex.[32] Driving licence controls were introduced to improve traffic safety and assist the movement of persons, either for those settling in a member state other than the one in which they reside or for more general movement within the Community.

Driving licences are now regulated by Directive 91/439.[33] The Community driving licence, in the form of a plastic card, was introduced in 1996.[34] The plastic 'credit-card' type licences are optional. Member states are free to continue to issue their paper licences. However, the information included on all licences must be the same and the new type of licence must be recognized throughout the Community. The Directive lists the types of vehicles which the holder of the driving licence is authorized to drive (Art. 3). Conditions imposed on the holder must be stated on the licence (Art. 4). Minimum age conditions for the issue of various categories of vehicles are specified (Art. 6).

---

[31] OJ 1994 L 319/7, adapted to technical progress by Commission Directive 96/86, OJ 1996 L 335/43. The Directive repeals Directive 89/684, OJ 1989 L 398/33, on vocational training for certain drivers of vehicles carrying dangerous goods by road.

[32] Directive 80/1263, OJ 1980 L 375/1.

[33] OJ 1991 L 237/1, last amended by Directive 97/26, OJ 1997 L 150/41.

[34] Directive 96/47, OJ 1996 L 235/1.

In June 1998 the Convention on Driving Disqualifications was signed, imposing an obligation on the member state of residence of the licence holder to give effect to driving disqualifications imposed by another member state. The member state of residence is obliged to take measures entailing the withdrawal, suspension or cancellation of the driving licence.[35]

A number of measures concerning lorry speed limits have been enacted. The beneficial effects of speed limitation devices on the protection of the environment and on road safety underpins these measures. Directive 92/6[36] requires the installation of speed-limiting devices in certain specified categories of vehicles having a maximum design speed exceeding 25 km/h (Art. 1): a maximum speed for coaches of 100km/h and for lorries of 90 km/h (Arts 2 and 3). Directive 92/24[37] sets out in annexes the requirements for EC-type approval of speed-limiting devices.

Reduction: harmonization of safety measures

Specific legislation has been enacted to regulate the transportation of dangerous goods by road. Directive 94/55[38] approximates the laws of the member states concerning the international and national transportation of dangerous goods by road. As stated above, Directive 94/55 transposed into Community law and implemented international rules governing the transport of dangerous goods. The Directive determines, with reference to ADR, the dangerous goods for which road haulage will be prohibited as well as those for which transport by road may be authorized (Art. 3). The authorization is subject to compliance with certain conditions relating to packaging and labelling and stated standards as to construction and operation of the vehicle concerned (Art. 6). Provision is made for vehicles registered in non-Community countries which comply with the ADR to transport freely goods within the Community (Art. 7). A committee consisting of representatives of the member states was established to assist the Commission with proposals (Art. 9).

Once road checks of dangerous goods at frontiers were abolished it was necessary to coordinate checks by member states inside their territory in order to ensure these were not excessive, discriminatory or insufficient. Directive 95/50[39] requires member states to ensure a 'representative pro-

---

[35] OJ 1998 C 216/1.
[36] OJ 1992 L 57/27.
[37] OJ 1992 L 129/154.
[38] See n. 31 above.
[39] OJ 1995 L 249/35 – proposal for amendment COM (2000) 106.

portion' of road haulage of dangerous goods will be subject to checks set down in an indicative list in order to verify conformity with the legislation (Art. 3(1)). Checks should be carried out in accordance with Art. 3 of Regulation 4060/89, which eliminates controls performed at frontiers.[40] The checks should not exceed a 'reasonable' length of time, be carried out at random and, as far as possible, cover an extensive part of the road network. A sample of the goods transported may be taken for examination (Art. 4).

Where any of the prescribed indicative safety standards is infringed (e.g. no danger labels, or the driver being without the appropriate certificate), the vehicle must be immobilized until made safe (Art. 5). Member states are required to grant each other assistance for the correct implementation of the Directive, notably notifying the carrier's home state in the cases of serious or repeated infractions committed by non-resident vehicles or undertakings (Art. 7). Member states are also required to provide returns to the Commission giving complete details of infringements committed and penalties imposed on resident and non-resident EC carriers and by non-Community carriers. Action taken by the home member state in response to the infringements recorded in other member states is also to be communicated to the Commission (Art. 9).

Technical safety standards and the testing of vehicles have also concerned the Community. A large number of Community measures have been adopted harmonizing national laws in respect of technical safety measures concerning vehicles and their trailers. Often a Council directive is adopted which empowers the Commission to adapt these basic directives to technical progress. These include, for example: measures on compulsory safety belts;[41] on the interior fittings of motor vehicles (strength of seats and their anchorages);[42] on the installation of lighting and light-signalling;[43] on retro-reflectors;[44] on lamps;[45] on the reverse and speedometer equipment;[46] on braking devices of certain categories;[47] and on steering equipment.[48]

Directive 89/459,[49] for example, aligns national legislation on tyre tread

---

40 OJ 1989 L 390/18. See Chapter 3 for further details.
41 Directive 91/671, OJ 1991 L 373/26.
42 Commission Directive 96/37 OJ 1996 L 186/28.
43 Commission Directive 97/28, OJ 1997 L 171/1.
44 Commission Directive 97/29, OJ 1997 L 171/11.
45 Commission Directive 97/30, OJ 1997 L 171/25.
46 Commission Directive 97/39, OJ 1997 L 177/15.
47 Commission Directive 98/12, OJ 1998 L 81/1.
48 Commission Directive 99/7, OJ 1997 L 40/36.
49 OJ 1989 L 226/4.

depths. A minimum tyre tread depth of 1.6 mm is now compulsory (Art. 1). A derogation is provided for vehicles of historical interest as long as these vehicles are hardly ever used on public roads (Art. 2). Similar legislation, mostly adopted in 1993, harmonized the standards for various parts of two- and three-wheeled vehicles.

As far as testing standards are concerned, Directive 96/96[50] amends and consolidates into a single text earlier legislation which regulated periodic roadworthiness tests for motor vehicles and their trailers. These annual tests are to be carried out by the member state or by national designated bodies and directly supervised by the state (Art. 2). Each member state is to test vehicles registered in that state in accordance with the Directive (Art. 1). The tests are to be recognized by the other member states (Art. 3(2)). Some derogations are permitted, such as for armed forces vehicles (Art. 4).

Annual roadworthiness tests are considered not to be sufficient to guarantee that those vehicles tested are in a roadworthy condition throughout the year. An amended proposal for a Directive has been published to provide for additional roadside inspections to ensure that heavy vehicles weighing over 3.5 tonnes and coaches using Community roads meet Community technical and safety requirements.[51] The measure will apply to heavy vehicles registered in a non-Community country. The proposed directive suggests that member states carry out spot checks on a 'representative cross-section' of commercial vehicles on their roads each year.

Protection of the environment

The Commission's strategy for integrating transport and the environment was set out in a 1998 working paper on 'environmental problems connected with lorry traffic'. The concept of the 'greener lorry' has influenced Community policy towards facilitating combined transport: road/rail or road/inland waterway. The working paper identifies the following issues for action: developing infrastructures and rail services; finding a solution to the problem of relating transport charges to actual road use, the weight of lorries, etc.; encouraging combined rail/road transport; improvement of technical standards of vehicles (construction and technical controls); and settling of the problems in the Alps.

As far as specific environmental matters are concerned, several directives have been adopted concerning air and sound pollution. Regarding air pollution, Directive 70/220,[52] frequently amended, limits values for carbon

---

[50] OJ 1996 L 46/1, as amended.
[51] COM (99) 458 final.
[52] OJ 1970 L 76/1, subsequently amended.

monoxide and unburnt hydrocarbon emissions from the engines of motor vehicles. Following the Commission's 1998 report on reduction of CO2 emissions, a proposal[53] for a directive broadening the scope of Directive 88/77 (on emissions)[54] is under discussion. The amendment seeks to keep standards for heavy vehicles parallel with those already in place for private cars. Directive 70/157,[55] as amended, approximates the laws of the member states relating to the permissible sound level and the exhaust system of vehicles. The Directive explicitly specifies the testing process.

Railways

As far as railway transport is concerned, measures have been adopted on safety certificates and with regard to the transport of dangerous goods by rail.

Safety certificates (Directive 95/19)

Directive 95/19[56] requires member states to award safety certificates to railway undertakings meeting certain requirements. The certificate will be issued to the undertaking when it complies with regulations under national law (compatible with Community law) on technical and operational regulations, on safety requirements applying to staff, on rolling stock and on the undertakings' internal organization. In particular the undertaking must provide proof that the staff whom it employs to operate the trains have the necessary training and meet safety regulations. The rolling stock must have been approved by the public authority or by the infrastructure manager (Art. 11).

Dangerous goods (Directive 96/49)

Directive 96/49[57] was adopted on the approximation of national laws with regard to the transport of dangerous goods by rail. The Directive seeks to extend the provisions of the Convention on International Carriage by Rail (RID) to the carriage of dangerous goods within member states or between member states. The provisions of the Directive are similar to those described above in respect of road transport.

---

53 COM (98) 204.
54 OJ 1998 L 36/33.
55 OJ 1970 L 42/16, last amended by Directive 92/97, OJ 1992 L 371/1 and adapted to technical progress by Commission Directive 96/20, OJ 1996 L 92/23.
56 OJ 1995 L 143/75. See Chapter 3 for other aspects of the Directive.
57 OJ 1996 L 235/25.

Inland waterways

As far as inland waterway transport is concerned, measures have been adopted on the reciprocal recognition of national boatmasters' certificates, on the harmonization of conditions for obtaining the certificates, on the carriage of dangerous goods and on safety inspections.

Professional competence: boatmasters' certificates (Directive 91/672)

The first step towards common provisions on the sailing of inland waterway vessels was taken by the adoption of Directive 91/672[58] on the reciprocal recognition of national boatmasters' certificates for the carriage of goods and passengers (listed in Annex I). However, differences in national legislation relating to the conditions for obtaining boatmasters' certificates remained until the adoption of Directive 96/50.[59]

Directive 91/672 approaches reciprocity by subdividing national certificates into Group A, meaning those which are valid for waterways of a maritime character (listed in Annex II) and Group B, being those valid for other Community waterways with the exception of the Rhine, the Lek and the Waal (Art. 1). The Rhine navigation licences issued in accordance with the Revised Rhine Navigation Convention are valid for all Community waterways without any derogation (Art. 2).

Member states are to recognize each other's certificates but recognition may be made subject to the same minimum age conditions as those laid down in the host member state for the same group. Recognition may also be limited to those categories of vessels for which the certificate is valid in the home member state. Provision is also made for member states, subject to consultation with the Commission, to require that, for the purpose of navigation of certain waterways other than waterways of a maritime character, boatmasters from other member states satisfy additional conditions concerning knowledge of the local situation equivalent to those required for its national boatmasters (Art. 3(3) to (5)).

Directive 96/50 not only seeks to remove national differences relating to the conditions for obtaining boatmasters' certificates but also to make safety requirements in the inland navigation gradually stricter. The Directive provides for a model for a single national boatmasters' certificate (Art. 1(1)) for operation in navigable waterways linked to the navigable network of another member state. The Directive does not affect the existing provisions concerning the Rhine navigation licence (Art. 1(5)). Member

---

[58] OJ 1991 L 373/29.
[59] OJ 1996 L 235/31.

states may, after consulting the Commission, exempt from the scope of the Directive licences for boatmasters operating exclusively on national waterways not linked to those of other member states (Art. 3(2)).

The conditions for issuing the certificate establish the minimum requirements which the applicant must meet. These requirements concern age (Art. 5), the physical and mental fitness of the applicants (Art. 6), their professional experience (Art. 7) and knowledge of certain subjects relating to the sailing vessels (Art. 8). Member states may, in the interests of safety, impose additional requirements regarding the knowledge of certain local situations (Art. 8(2)). Additional professional knowledge is required to navigate with the aid of radar or to sail a vessel carrying passengers (Arts 9 and 10).

Dangerous goods (Directive 82/714)

Directive 82/714[60] provides that a certificate issued pursuant to the Regulation for the Transport of Dangerous Substances on the Rhine (ADNR) permits the carriage of dangerous goods throughout the territory of the Community (Art. 6). A member state may require that vessels which do not carry an ADNR certificate be authorized to carry dangerous goods within its territory only if the vessels comply with the requirements additional to those set out in the Directive.

An amended proposal for a directive approximating the laws of the member states in respect of the transport of dangerous goods by vessels on inland waterways has been published.[61] The measure, whose objective is to transpose into Community law the UN recommendation on the international carriage of dangerous goods by inland waterways, will complement similar ones which have been adopted for the transport of dangerous goods by road and rail.

The proposal recognizes that such transportation has considerably expanded and has thus increased the risks of accidents occurring. The proposal contains provisions on training requirements for the crews of vessels transporting dangerous goods. Provision is made to allow member states to remain free to regulate such traffic in certain waterways not covered by the proposed Directive as well as to derogate in respect of ferry operations undertaken solely for the purpose of crossing an inland waterway or a harbour area in order to take into account the local character and the wide range of different types of ferry boats.

---

[60] OJ 1982 OJ L 301/1. See also Chapter 3.
[61] COM (99) 563 final.

Inspections (Directive 82/714)

Directive 82/714 provides for competent national authorities to check at any time that a vessel is carrying a valid certificate (Art. 17(1)). If the authorities find that the certificate is invalid (or that the vessel does not satisfy the requirements set out in the certificate) but that no manifest danger exists, the owner of the vessel or his representative must take all necessary measures to remedy the situation (Art. 17(2)). However, if the authorities find that the certificate is not being carried or that the vessel constitutes a manifest danger, they may prevent the vessel from proceeding until the necessary steps have been taken to remedy the situation (Art. 17(3)). Such a decision has to be reasoned and subject to appeal (Art. 17(5)).

Provision is also made for the member state concerned to inform the authorities in the member state which issued or last renewed the certificate, of the decision it has taken or intends to take (Art. 17(4)).

As far as inspection of shipping on the Rhine is concerned, the matter is governed by its own regulation.

Maritime transport

Background

Safety is a major concern for this industry not only within the Community but world-wide and this has resulted in a number of international Conventions being negotiated and signed under the auspices of the International Maritime Organisation (IMO). Community maritime safety policy has been mainly built on the basis of IMO Conventions. The Community adopts measures urging member states to ratify these Conventions but often resorts to adopting legislation which incorporates the internationally agreed standards. These standards then become binding on the member states as Community law. In enacting legislation the Community has been spurred on by major accidents at sea which have endangered life and/or the environment; on these occasions Community measures have often been stricter than international standards.

In 1978, for example, in response to the *Amico Cadiz* disaster, Recommendations were adopted urging member states to ratify international Conventions on safety, prevention of pollution from ships and concerning standards of training, certification and watchkeeping for seafarers.[62] In the late 1980s, in response to the 1987 *Herald of Free*

---

[62] Recommendations: 78/684, OJ 1978 L 194/17 (1974 Convention for the Safety of Life at Sea (SOLAS) plus its 1978 Protocol and 1976 ILO Convention No. 147 concerning mini-

Enterprise disaster, attention was given to the safety of roll-on/roll-off (Ro-Ro) ferries.[63] In 1993, in response to the *Estonia* ferry disaster, the Council adopted a Resolution supporting the Commission Communication entitled 'A Common Policy on Safe Seas', which listed the measures to be taken by the Community and the member states to enhance maritime safety and pollution prevention.[64] Specific measures were then adopted on matters such as the minimum level of training of seafarers, common standards for classification societies, ship inspections and surveys, port state control, transportation of dangerous goods and passenger safety. The *Erika* tanker disaster at the end of 1999 has once again resulted in the Commission proposing to strengthen existing legislation in this area.[65]

Training and professional competence (Directives 79/115 and 94/58)

As far as seamen are concerned, no special provisions have been enacted: their rights are the same as for any other workers who are nationals of a member state and are governed by Art. 39 EC Treaty and Regulation 1612/68.[66] In the context of maritime transport seamen are free to move from ships flying the flag of a member state to ships registered under the flag of another member state. In practice, however, there are still restrictions. Officers, particularly captains, are regarded as having a dual role. They are not only representatives of the state whose flag the ship sails under, but captains, in particular, have also a public function (e.g. performance of marriages) and are probably excluded from the application of these provisions, since Art. 39, para. 4, provides that 'the provisions of this Article do not apply with regard to employment in the public service'. The position of officers, other than captains, is less certain and more likely to be outside the scope of the public service exception. As far as seamen are concerned, problems also arise from the non-recognition of seamen's diplomas and certificates of competence. However, Directive 89/48,[67] on a general recognition system for higher education diplomas issued after training of at least three years, will cover some of the professions exercised on board ship.

---

mum standards in merchant ships); 79/114, OJ 1979 L 33/31 (Convention on Standards of Training, Certification and Watchkeeping for Seafarers); 79/487, OJ 1979 L 125/18 (1977 Convention for Safe Containers (CSC)); 80/907, OJ 1980 L 259/29 (1977 Torremolinos Convention for the Safety of Fishing Vessels).

[63] Passenger ships which provide horizontal means of access for cars and other vehicles.

[64] OJ 1993 C 271/1.

[65] COM (2000) 142 final, proposal to amend Directive 94/57, see below.

[66] Sp. Ed. 1968 No. L 257/2 p. 475.

[67] OJ 1989 L 19/16.

Directive 79/115[68] was adopted in respect of deep-sea pilots in the North Sea and English Channel with two aims. First, to ensure that pilots are adequately qualified and, secondly, to encourage ships navigating these heavily used waterways to employ such pilots and not to cut costs by using less qualified crew. The Directive, however, does not require the shipowner or master to use the services of a deep-sea pilot. The Directive imposed obligations on the member states with coasts bordering on the North Sea and English Channel to take all necessary and appropriate measures to ensure that such qualified pilots were available and on all member states to encourage ships flying their flag to use such services (Art. 1).

Directive 94/58[69] on minimum level of training for seafarers is based on the international rules defined in the IMO Convention on Standards of Training, Certification and Watchkeeping for Seafarers (STCW Convention). The Directive applies to seafarers serving on board seagoing ships flying a member state flag except warships (or ships operated only for government non-commercial service), fishing boats, wooden ships of primitive build and pleasure yachts not engaged in trade (Art. 1). Member states are required to ensure that all seafarers are trained and hold a certificate of aptitude issued by a member state and in accordance with IMO rules (Arts 2, 3 and 5). An obligation is imposed on member states to designate an authority responsible for the training, examining and issuing of certificates of competence (Art. 7). Provision is also made for national competent authorities, in circumstances of exceptional necessity, to issue dispensations. These are limited to a period of not exceeding six months and must not cause danger to persons, property or the environment (Art. 6).

Member states are permitted, within the context of port state control, to detain a ship if crews are unable to provide proof of the professional competence required (Art. 11). Ships flying a flag of a non-Community country which has not ratified the STCW Convention or which carry certificates not recognized by Community law are to be inspected as a matter of priority (Art. 10). The 1995 revised requirements of the STCW Convention have been incorporated into Community law and, therefore, a common criteria for recognition of the seafarers' certificate issued by the administrations of non-Community states have been established (Art. 9(3) and (4), as amended). Provisions for a working language for crew communication on board Ro-Ro passenger ships has also been incorporated (Art. 8).

---

[68] OJ 1979 L 33/32.
[69] OJ 1994 L 319/28, subsequently amended by Directive 98/35, OJ 1998 L 172/1, to incorporate the 1995 substantial modifications made to the STCW Convention.

Certification: classification societies (Directive 94/57)

Directive 94/57[70] establishes common rules and quality standards which should be observed by member states and by the organizations in charge of inspections, verification and certification of ships. The Directive seeks to ensure compliance with international Conventions and therefore remove all substandard ships from Community waters (Art. 1).

Member states must ensure that their competent authorities can guarantee appropriate enforcement and so they may entrust these tasks only to recognized classification societies (Art. 3). A working relationship must be established between the relevant national authorities and the classification societies authorized to act on their behalf (Art. 6).

Classification societies may only be recognized if they meet the criteria set out in the annex to the Directive (Art. 4). For example, the approved body must be able to justify extensive experience in assessing design and construction of merchant ships and publish, on annual basis, their register. Thus it is required that ships with a total weight of at least 5,000,000 grt must be registered with the society, which must employ at least 100 inspectors (i.e. technical surveyors). The society must also be independent of shipowners or shipbuilders and have comprehensive rules and regulations for the design, construction and periodic inspection (survey) of merchant ships, published and continually upgraded and improved through research and development programmes. Provision is also made for the suspension or withdrawal of recognition (Art. 9) and for monitoring to ensure that the recognized societies continue to meet the criteria (Art. 11).

If a task is entrusted to a recognized classification society in a non-Community state, the member states may request reciprocal recognition (Art. 5(3)). Ships certified by a society which is not included in the Community's list[71] will be selected for priority port inspection in order to verify whether they meet IMO standards (Art. 12(1)).

Member states have an obligation to ensure ships flying their flag are constructed and maintained in accordance with the requirement of a recognized classification society (Art. 14).

Ships: fishing boats and passenger ships (Directives 97/70 and 98/18)

Directive 97/70[72] sets up harmonized safety standards for sea-going fishing ships of 24 metres or more in length. The measure primarily extends the

---

[70] OJ 1994 L 319/20, subsequently amended.
[71] Commission Decision 96/587, OJ 1996 L 257/43, subsequently amended.
[72] OJ 1997 L 34/1, subsequently amended.

1977 Torremolinos Convention for the Safety of Fishing Vessels (and its 1993 Protocol) to ships between 24 and 45 metres in length sailing under the flag of a member state or operating in the domestic waters or territorial sea of a member state or unloading their catches in a port of a member state (Art. 1).

The Convention and Protocol deal in particular with the certification, construction and equipment of fishing boats, their stability, machines and gear, fire prevention, protection of the crew, safety provisions, emergency procedures, radio communication and navigation equipment.

The Directive does not apply to recreational craft engaged in non-commercial fishing. Provision is made for member states requiring specific safety measures due to local circumstances or the ships' particulars (Art. 4). The design, construction and maintenance of the hull and other matters concerning the ship shall be according to the rules in force at the date of construction. Rules for new ships shall be in accordance with Directive 94/57(Art. 5). Certificates of compliance shall be issued by the flag state (Art. 6). For those fishing boats flying non-Community flags, provision is made for existing control measures also to apply (e.g. port state control) (Art. 7). Provision is included for penalties to be imposed where a breach of national law adopted pursuant to the Directive has occurred (Art. 11).

As far as passenger ships are concerned, the relevant measure is Directive 98/18[73] on safety rules and standards for passenger ships. The main objective of the measure is to make compliance with the rules of the SOLAS (Safety at Sea) Convention, which applies only to international voyages, compulsory for all ships sailing in Community waters. Thus it extends the Convention rules to passenger ships operating in the national waters of member states.

The Directive applies to new and existing passenger ships and to high speed passenger craft regardless of their flag when engaged on domestic voyages (Art. 3(1)). Member states cannot exclude from operation ships when engaged on domestic voyages, which comply with the requirements of the Directive (Art. 5(2)). However, a host member state (a member state of departure or of destination) may inspect such ships in accordance with the Port State Control Directive. In addition, the host member state may participate in investigations into accidents affecting regular services in their ports.

Passenger ships are divided into classes according to the sea area in which they operate (Art. 4(1)). Specific safety requirements for new and

---

[73] OJ 1998 L 144/1.

existing ships are specified for each class of ship (Art. 6). Provision is made for additional safety requirements where member states consider them necessary due to specific local circumstances. Similar provision is included for exemptions from certain specific requirements where the local conditions so permit. In either case the member state concerned has to notify and obtain the approval of the European Commission. Commission approval is also necessary where a member state considers it necessary to adopt safeguard measures (Art. 7).

An obligation is imposed on the administration of the flag state to carry out initial and periodical surveys of ships put into service (Art. 10). A passenger ship Safety Certificate of Compliance with the Directive must be issued for a period not exceeding 12 months (Art. 11). Penalties are also to be imposed for breach of national laws adopted in pursuance of the Directive.

Dangerous goods (Directive 93/75)

Directive 93/75[74] concerns the minimum requirements for ships (not warships or other official ships) bound for or leaving Community ports and carrying dangerous or polluting goods. The main objective is to improve prevention and remedial action in the event of circumstances at sea which might lead to accidents (Art. 6). The Directive seeks to ensure that member states' competent authorities are informed of the presence of dangerous or polluting goods on board ships (Art. 1). No dangerous or polluting goods may be transported unless a declaration has been delivered to the master or operator containing the correct technical names of the goods, the United Nations numbers where they exist, the IMO hazard classes in accordance with international codes and the quantities of such goods (Art. 4). The operator of the ship must notify specified information to the competent member state authority before departure. The operator of a ship coming from a non-Community port has similar obligations as a condition for the entry or anchorage into a Community port (Art. 5).

The Directive applies to tankers, the requirements for which will be more stringent than those laid down in Directive 79/116 on the entry into and departure from Community ports of this type of ship. Provision is made for exemptions to be granted either by the member state or by the Commission on request from a member state (Art. 5(4)).

The Directive has been extended[75] to cover carriage of irradiated nuclear

---

74 OJ 1993 L 247/19.
75 Directive 98/55, OJ 1998 L 215/65.

fuel, plutonium and high level radioactive waste in flasks on board ships. A proposal for a directive setting up a European vessels reporting system (Eurorep) has been under discussion for some time.[76] Directive 93/75 applies only in respect of information available at the time the ship leaves port. The new directive will fill the gap by requiring information on the movements of ships off the coasts of member states.

Regulation 259/93[77] was adopted on the supervision and control of shipments of waste within, into and out of the Community. The measure establishes a regime whereby shipments of waste need to comply with a minimum criteria to ensure that human health and the environment are protected.

A further directive is proposed to reduce ship-generated waste and cargo residues in all Community ports. Strict rules will be adopted to ensure adequate rejection facilities will be provided in all Community ports including recreational ports and marinas and will require all ships, fishing boats and recreational craft visiting these ports to make use of the facilities provided.

Passenger safety (Directive 98/41)

Following the *Estonia* ferry disaster, a safety scheme was established that is common to all Ro-Ro ferries and high speed passenger craft sailing regularly to and from Community ports irrespective of the flag they fly. In 1994 the Council adopted a Resolution on Safety of Ro-Ro[78] to enhance passenger safety on these ferries by improving their design and equipment, the quality of their crews and the responsibility of owners and operators of this type of ship. As many ships currently operating such services are flagged out, that is registered in a non-Community state, and thus do not automatically fall under the jurisdiction of member states, a regime for verification and inspection to ensure compliance was needed. It was also necessary for host member states to participate in any investigation of maritime accidents or casualties.

The Resolution was followed by the adoption of Regulation 3051/95[79] bringing forward by two years the application of the IMO Code on International Safety Management (ISM Code) for Ro-Ro ferries operating regular services to and from Community ports. Regulation 3051/95 lays down the necessary provisions to improve safety at sea and to prevent

---

[76] COM (94) 220 final.
[77] OJ 1993 L 30/1.
[78] OJ 1994 C 379/8.
[79] OJ 1995 L 320/14, subsequently amended by Commission Regulation 179/98, OJ 1998 L 19/35, to introduce the relevant parts of the ISM Guidelines for administrators.

marine pollution by obliging the shipping companies to establish and maintain adequate safety management systems on board and on land.

The measure applies to all companies operating at least one Ro-Ro ferry on a regular service to and from Community ports regardless of flag. Shipping companies are required to comply with the ISM Code and only upon compliance will they be authorized to operate Ro-Ro ferries.

Flag states are obliged to certify compliance by issuing a Safety Management Certificate. After consulting the administration of the flag state, member states must issue a Document of Compliance for shipping companies which have their principal place of business on their territory. The validity of the two documents is limited to five years. Member states are obliged to recognize Documents of Compliance and Safety Management Certificates issued by authorities of non-Community states where they guarantee compliance with the provisions of this Regulation.

Provision is made for a member state, for reasons of serious danger to safety or the environment, to suspend the operation of a service and bring the matter before the European Commission.

A further development was the adoption of Directive 98/41[80] introducing a compulsory passenger registration system on passenger ships (except warships, troopships and pleasure yachts) operating to or from Community ports (Art. 3). The aim of the measure is to help search teams in case of accidents to know exactly how many people were travelling and to identify victims speedily (Art. 1). The Directive makes it compulsory for all shipping authorities to count the passengers on all domestic and international voyages as well as to record their name, sex and age on journeys over 20 miles. This information must be obtained before the ship departs from a Community port (Arts 4 and 5). This measure ensures that the number of passengers does not exceed the ship's capacity and that, in the event of an accident, rescue services will know exactly how many people will require assistance. An express obligation is imposed on the master of a ship to make sure that the number of passengers on board does not exceed the number the passenger ship is permitted to carry (Art. 7). Obligations are also imposed on shipping companies operating passenger ships to set up a system of registration and to appoint a passenger registrar responsible for keeping and transmitting the information (Art. 8). The registration systems must meet the following functional criteria: readability; accessibility; readiness; facilitation; security; and alternative means.

Derogations and exemptions are permitted though limited. Member states may lower the 20-mile threshold and may exempt passenger ships

---

[80] OJ 1998 L 188/35.

operating in sheltered waters on scheduled services from some or all of the obligations mentioned in the Directive but under specified conditions.

Port state control and inspections (Directive 95/21)

As far as port state control is concerned, Directive 95/21[81] (the Port State Control Directive) establishes a legal framework of harmonized control procedures with the aim of reducing the perceived high incidence of substandard ships operating in Community waters. The measure seeks to strengthen the effectiveness of the Memorandum of Understanding on Port State Control signed in Paris in 1982 by 15 European maritime administrations.

Thus the measure has two objectives: first, to tighten up inspections of all merchant ships and crews using Community ports and navigating in Community waters; and secondly, to impose a strict adherence to the international standards adopted in respect of maritime safety, pollution prevention and living and working conditions on board (Art. 1).

The Directive applies to any ship and its crew calling at or anchored off a Community port or an off-shore installation. It does not apply to fishing boats, warships or pleasure yachts not engaged in trade (Art. 3).

An obligation is imposed on member states to establish and maintain national maritime administrations ('competent authorities') for the inspection of ships in their ports or in waters under their jurisdiction (Art. 4). Each member state is under an obligation to inspect at least 25% of the ships which entered their ports in the previous year (Art. 5). No further inspection will be carried out on ships which have been inspected within the previous six months. These inspections have to conform to a common criteria on the selection of ships, control procedures for rectification and for the detention of ships. A list of certificates and documents to be inspected and the types of inspection to be carried out is laid down together with the rules to be followed if a more detailed inspection provides necessary (Arts 6 to 8).

Member states are to ensure that any deficiencies revealed in the course of the inspection are rectified and conditions warranting detention of the ship are laid down (Art. 9). The conditions to be met in order to allow a ship to proceed to a repair yard are also laid down. Penalties may be imposed in the event of refusal to comply with the competent authorities' requests including refusal of access to any port within the Community (Art. 11).

---

[81] OJ 1995 L 157/1, subsequently amended and already mentioned above.

The Directive also lays down rules on the professional competence and qualification criteria for the inspectors (Art. 12).[82] Every three years member states have to supply details of the number of inspectors working on their behalf and of the number of ships entering their ports (Art. 17).

Directive 95/21 has been amended to incorporate stricter standards resulting from amendments to major maritime Conventions (MARPOL, SOLAS and STCW).[83] For example, port state control authorities are required to check the implementation of the International Management Code for Safe Operation of Ships (ISM Code) on board all ships.[84]

Protection of the environment

It was only as late as 1978, following the damage caused by the *Amoco Cadiz* incident off the coast of Brittany, that the Community took the initiative by adopting Recommendation 78/584[85] urging member states to ratify a number of international Conventions which included the 1973 Convention (and its 1978 Protocol) for the prevention of pollution by ships (MARPOL). Soon after, Directive 79/116[86] was adopted on minimum requirements for certain tankers entering or leaving Community ports, thus reducing the risk of consequential oil pollution.

Directive 79/116 applies not only to oil, gas and chemical tankers of 1,600 grt and over (fully or partly laden) but also to tankers which, although empty, have not yet been degassed or purged of hazardous residues (Art. 1). Before such tankers enter a port of a member state, competent national authorities must be given specific minimum information as stated in Art. 1(A). The information includes the nature of the cargo, port of destination and nationality. Article 1(B) provides a similar list of matters to be notified to the competent national authorities when tankers are traversing the territorial waters adjacent to the port of entry or departure. Information must also be communicated to the authorities of any deficiency potentially dangerous to the safety of shipping and to the marine environment. Pilots are required to inform the authorities of any deficiencies (Art. 1(2)). Further, the Directive imposes an obligation on the member states in receipt of information which involves an increased risk

---

[82] Commission Directive 96/40, OJ 1996 L 196/8, establishes a common model for an identity card for port state control inspectors as referred to in Art. 12(4) of Directive 95/21.

[83] Directive 98/25, OJ 1998 L 133/19.

[84] The Code requires ships to have on board a 'Safety Management Certificate' and a copy of the 'Document of Compliance' in which the flag state approves the safety management system of the ship and of the company respectively.

[85] OJ 1978 L 194/17.

[86] OJ 1979 L 33/33.

for another member state to inform that other member state (Art. 2). A tanker check list is annexed to the Directive to assist in providing the fuller information required.

Regulation 2978/94[87] is aimed at promoting 'friendly' oil tankers in transport operations to, from or within the Community by implementing IMO Resolution A.747(18) on the tonnage measurement of ballast spaces in segregated ballast oil tankers (SBTs). The measure seeks to remove the prejudice in relation to port fees which arises where dues are calculated on the basis of gross tonnage. The text envisaged two possibilities, either the deduction of the space taken by the segregated ballast tanks from the gross tonnage, or ensuring that the fee for an SBT is at least 17% lower than that applicable to a non-SBT of the same gross weight. Where fees are assessed other than on gross tonnage, port and pilotage authorities must ensure that SBTs receive treatment no less favourable than when fees are calculated in accordance with one or more of these methods.

Air transport

Background

Safety is of paramount importance in this industry. In 1998 the Council authorized the Commission to enter into negotiation for the creation of an European Aviation Safety Authority (EASA) to oversee the development of more systematic methods of assessing the airworthiness of aircraft. The Commission has responded by proposing an European agency and not the Council's preferred option, an international organization.

In addition, the Commission's White Paper entitled 'Air Traffic Management – Freeing Europe's Air Space',[88] had already called for a single, coherent and uniform system to be set in place throughout Europe. It is suggested that a reconstructed Eurocontrol[89] is well placed to take on this regulatory role. The Community is seeking membership of Eurocontrol in its own right.

Professional competence (Directive 91/670)

Directive 91/670[90] lays down a procedure for mutual acceptance of personnel licences issued by member states to civil aviation cockpit personnel

---

[87] OJ 1994 L 319/1.
[88] COM (96) 57 final.
[89] Eurocontrol, the European Organization for Air Traffic Safety, is an inter-governmental organization for the security of air transport in Europe. It is also the air traffic control organization in Europe.
[90] OJ 1991 L 373/21.

(Art. 1). The Directive covers all licences authorizing the holder to exercise functions as a member of the cockpit personnel on board a civil aircraft registered in a member state (Art. 2). Provision is made for a member state to ask the Commission for an opinion on the equivalence of a licence presented to it for acceptances (Art. 4(2)). Member states are obliged to accept, without undue delay or additional tests, any licence issued by another member state together with privileges and certificates pertaining thereto (Art. 3). The Commission has delivered two opinions pursuant to Art. 4(2) of the Directive.[91]

A proposal for a Directive on safety requirements and attestation of professional competence for cabin crews is under discussion.[92]

Aviation accidents investigation (Directive 94/56)

Directive 94/56[93] was adopted establishing fundamental principles governing the investigation of civil aviation accidents and incidents. It seeks to improve air safety by facilitating the expeditious holding of investigations, the sole objective of which is the prevention of future accidents and incidents (Art. 1).

The measure provides for investigations to be carried out according to international norms (Annex 13 to the Chicago Convention) under the control of the state where the accident occurred. However, if that state fails to initiate such an investigation the state of the aircraft's registration may do so. The investigations are mandatory (Art. 4).

The Directive applies to accidents occurring in the Community and also to investigation of serious incidents involving aircraft registered in a member state or operated by an undertaking established in a member state, when such an investigation is not carried out by another non-Community country (Art. 2).

A clear separation between the judicial inquiry and the technical investigation is provided for, as well as a requirement for the investigation to be carried out by a permanent and independent body (Arts 5 and 6). The investigation of accidents or incidents must be subject to a report containing conclusions and eventual safety recommendations. Accident reports must be published but incident ones are only required to be circulated to the parties likely to benefit from its findings with regard to safety (Arts 7 and 8).

---

[91] OJ 1993 L 111/25 and L 267/29. Failure by Belgium to comply with the Directive has resulted in further action by the Commission.

[92] COM (99) 68 final.

[93] OJ 1994 L 319/14.

Certification and inspections (Regulation 3922/91)

Regulation 3922/91[94] addresses those aspects of aviation safety which relate to the airworthiness, operational approval and maintenance of aircraft, engines and other aircraft equipment. It was developed in consultation with the Joint Aviation Authorities (JAA) and other industry representative bodies. It makes existing international standards in this area (as listed in Annex II) legally binding in the Community (Art. 1). The Regulation is of a general nature and provides one of the major pillars on which the common air transport policy is founded. It applies to aircraft operated by undertakings registered in a member state or in a non-Community country. These undertakings may be natural or legal persons residing in a member state or a Community air carrier as defined in Community legislation. It covers certificates and approval granted by the national authorities or the bodies acting on their behalf to Community carriers.

Provision is made to enable a member state to react immediately to a safety problem which becomes apparent from an accident and involves a product which was designed, manufactured or maintained in accordance with the Regulation (Art. 8). As normal in this kind of legislation, provision is made for an amendment procedure to enable the adaptation to scientific and technical progress the requirements and procedures set out in Annex II (Art. 11). Finally, member states are obliged to be full members of the JAA (Art. 5).

A proposal for a directive is under discussion which aims at tightening safety checks carried out in Community airports on aircraft belonging to non-Community operators. The measure seeks to guarantee a high level of safety to all passengers using a Community airport.[95]

Protection of the environment

Several directives have been adopted to restrict or eliminate noisy aircraft from operating in the Community. Directive 80/51[96] fixes the limits on emissions of such noise, while Directive 89/629[97] prohibits the registration of new aircraft that only comply with the standards specified in Annex 16 of the Convention on International Civil Aviation (2nd ed., 1988), the so-called 'Chapter 2 aircraft'. This 'non-addition rule' was only the first stage

---

[94] OJ 1991 L 373/4.
[95] COM (98) 597 final.
[96] OJ 1980 L 18/26.
[97] OJ 1989 L 363/27.

in the process of eliminating noisy and old aircraft. Directive 92/14[98] seeks to restrict further the operation of such aircraft. Thus the Directive requires member states to register only aircraft which comply with the standards of Chapter 3 of Annex 16 (Art. 2) and provides a timetable for the gradual withdrawal from member states' registers of all aircraft not meeting Chapter 3 standards. A derogation until 2002 is permitted for aircraft from developing countries (Art. 3(b)). The Directive applies to aircraft with a maximum take-off mass of 34,000 kg or more and with a passenger capacity of 19 or more (Art. 1).

A controversial measure has been the adoption of Regulation 925/99[99] banning 'hush-kitted' (a kind of muffler which helps to reduce noise) aircraft from being added to member states' registers. The Regulation provides a non-addition rule for aircraft registered in the member states. The Regulation also bans from Community airports such aircraft registered in non-Community countries. For aircraft registered in non-Community countries the Directive provides equivalent requirements. This is achieved by recognizing for hush-kitted aircraft that have been operating at Community airports before 1 April 1999, the right to continue to fly into the Community after 1 April 2002. This right will last for as long as the aircraft remains on the register of the state where it was registered before 1 April 1999.[100]

The Commission has published a Communication entitled *Air Transport and the Environment: Towards meeting the Challenges of Sustainable Development*,[101] in which it outlines the proposed work programme for the next five years and beyond to handle the growth in aircraft emissions and airport congestion.

Passenger protection

Regulation 295/91[102] sets out common minimum standards of compensation for passengers denied boarding because the flight was overbooked ('bumped-off passengers'). The Regulation applies to all scheduled services operating from Community airports and thus not confined to Community

---

[98] OJ 1992 L 76/21.

[99] OJ 1999 L 115/1.

[100] The measure has been adopted to spur an international solution to the problem of aircraft noise. However, the US has objected to this measure since the using of hush-kits allows aircraft to be upgraded to Chapter 3 standard which complies with Directive 92/14 and the most stringent international noise standards. Thus the Community has agreed to delay its implementation until May 2000.

[101] COM (99) 640.

[102] OJ 1991 L 36/5.

carriers (Art. 1) but the measure does not cover non-scheduled flights nor flights from non-Community countries. The Regulation requires that each carrier must establish its own rules for denied boarding and make these rules available to the Commission, the member states and to the travelling public via travel agents and check-in counters (Art. 3). The Regulation obliges airlines to provide additional services to passengers who are denied boarding. It establishes a straightforward system of cash compensation irrespective of the price paid for the original ticket, although the total compensation offered need not exceed the price of that ticket. Compensation ranges from EUR 150 to 300 depending on the distance and length of delay involved (Art. 4).

Regulation 2027/97[103] has been adopted on air carrier liability in the event of accidents to passengers for damage sustained in the event of death or wounding (Art. 1). The Regulation sets out a liability scheme applicable to Community air carriers engaged in domestic or international operations. It provides better protection for passengers than that offered for international flights under the Warsaw Convention. The ceilings on compensation of the Warsaw Convention are waived and the Regulation provides for strict liability of up to EUR 100,000.

Technical requirements

Road transport

The basic Community measure on type-approval of motor vehicles and their trailers is Directive 70/156,[104] which approximated the relevant laws of member states. The Directive establishes an EC type-approval setting out specific requirements. It envisages separate directives being adopted, each containing an information document attached to it incorporating the relevant items of Annex I of the Directive and also a type-approval certificate in order that type approval may be computerized. For example, Directive 98/91[105] harmonizes the approval procedures in the member states of the means of transport of dangerous goods by road. The measure ensures the conformity of such vehicles with the requirements of the EC type-approval procedure established by Directive 70/156.

Weights and dimensions for lorries and buses have been gradually

---

[103] OJ 1997 L 285/1.
[104] OJ 1970 L 42/1, regularly amended.
[105] OJ 1998 L 11/25.

approximated and are currently regulated by Directive 96/53.[106] If vehicles over 3.5 tonnes comply with the limits specified in annexes in Community legislation, member states may not prohibit the use of such vehicles in their territory. This measure establishes uniform rules, not only for international transport, where this already existed, but also for national transport, in order to eliminate all distortion of competition in the progressive liberalization of cabotage. It allows for a maximum length of 18.75 metres, maximum width of 2.55 metres (also applied to buses) and a maximum authorized weight of 40 tonnes for six-axle vehicles.[107] Several other harmonization measures have been adopted which concern technical matters. These include measures on rear-view mirrors, type-approval certificates and brake devices. Similar measures have been adopted in respect of two- and three-wheeled motor vehicles.

Railways

One of the main goals of the Community's railway policy was to ensure technical harmonization and standardization, e.g. track gauge, signal systems. Thus Council Resolution 71/119[108] states the desirability of railway undertakings cooperating more in technical, commercial and administrative fields. Member states were requested to remove obstacles to such cooperation. However, effective action has only been taken with the adoption of Directive 96/48 on the interoperability of the trans-European high speed rail system.[109] The objective of the measure is to achieve interoperability within the Community by determining technical specifications for both railway lines and rolling stock so that high-speed trains may travel on all member states' networks (Art. 1). These trains are designed to travel at least 250 km/h but allowing for speeds over 300 km/h in some circumstances.

The Directive establishes a joint representative body comprising representatives of infrastructure managers, railway undertakings and equipment manufacturers to work out technical specifications for interoperability (TIS) as and when requested by the Commission. In some circumstances member states will be allowed not to apply the TIS (Art. 7).

---

[106] OJ 1996 L 235/59, amending and consolidating into a single text Directive 85/3, OJ 1985 L 2/14 and its subsequent amendments as well as Directive 86/364, OJ 1986 L 221/48 on proof of compliance.

[107] COM (2000) 137 proposes an increase to 44 tonnes for vehicles used in combined transport.

[108] OJ 1971 C 5/1.

[109] OJ 1996 L 235/6.

As with other technical harmonization measures, the Directive provides a procedure for an approved organization to award a 'CE' declaration of conformity for network components such as lines, rolling stock, signals and communication systems. Essential requirements for safety, environmental protection and technical compatibility are defined in the Directive.

A distinction is made in the Directive between new lines specifically designed for high-speed trains and lines that have been upgraded (Annex I). Although the former must allow trains to travel at speeds of 250 km/h and over, the latter may restrict them to 200 km/h. Rolling stock has to be designed to reach 300 km/h in the best circumstances and 250 km/h or more on new lines in other circumstances.

Inland waterways

Directive 76/135[110] on reciprocal recognition of navigability licences required common provisions establishing technical requirements for inland waterway vessels to be established. This was achieved by Directive 82/714,[111] which also provides a streamlined amendment procedure to facilitate the speedy adaptation to technical progress technical requirements set out in annexes. Annex II lays down the minimum technical requirements for vessels operating within the scope of the Directive. These range from requirements in respect of shipbuilding, machinery and electrical installations to health and safety in the crew's accommodation and working stations.

Maritime transport

Council Decision 92/143[112] was adopted on radio navigation systems for Europe. The measure seeks the highest degree of safety of navigation and protection of the marine equipment. It requires member states which participate in or join regional agreements to do so in a way which fulfils international obligations and to achieve radio navigation configurations which cover the widest possible geographical area in Europe and neighbouring waters (Art. 1). The Commission is also given a role in ensuring compatibility of systems, in particular, in the development of satellite navigation systems, existing terrestrial systems and of the radio navigation plans of the member states (Art. 2).

Directive 96/98[113] on maritime equipment is aimed at guaranteeing that all equipment for vessels sold in the Community conforms to common

---

110 OJ 1976 L 21/10. See also Chapter 3.
111 OJ 1982 L 301/1.
112 OJ 1992 L 59/17.
113 OJ 1996 L 46/25, subsequently amended.

international standards of safety, reliability and performance, so as to reduce the risk of maritime accidents (Art. 1). The Directive applies to equipment for use on board of any new Community ship, wherever the ship is situated at the time of construction, and to equipment placed on board existing Community ships, whether for the first time or to replace equipment already carried on board. It does not apply to equipment already on board (Art. 3). The Directive is based on the principle that member states bear responsibility for the safe management of their fleets. An obligation is imposed on each member state, when issuing or reviewing the relevant safety certificates, to ensure that equipment on board of ships flying its flag complies with the requirements of the Directive (Art. 4). The Directive ensures that compliance with international Conventions is compulsory (Art. 5). Member states cannot refuse recognition to equipment complying with the Directive (Art. 6).

Procedures are set out for establishing detailed testing standards for the equipment listed in an annex to the Directive and for evaluating equipment on board ships (Arts 10 to 13). The Commission and other member states are to be notified of organizations appointed by a member state to check conformity, indicating the specific tasks delegated and the identification numbers assigned to them (Art. 9).

The measure also contains provisions governing the placing on the market of totally new equipment (Art. 14) and the rules governing the replacement of equipment in a non-Community port in exceptional circumstances where it is impossible to find equipment which has been EC-type examined (Art. 16).

Air transport

No measures have been adopted except for Directive 93/65[114] on the definition and use of compatible technical specifications for the procurement of air-traffic-management equipment and systems.

Concluding observations

Much has been achieved in the 1990s to harmonize national laws so as to ensure minimum standards, and therefore access to the single market. In the maritime and air transport sectors a serious attempt has been made to ensure that international agreed standards are applied throughout the Community, both by undertakings established in a member state or by those whose ships and aircraft use Community ports and airports.

---

[114]   OJ 1993 L 187/52.

CHAPTER 6

Combined transport and infrastructure

Introduction

Combined transport has been perceived for a long time as an environmentally friendly solution to some of the problems facing the Community in providing for a suitable and safe infrastructure. However, the development of combined transport has been hindered by lack of suitable infrastructures and the incompatability of the various modes of transport. The objective in this area is to develop a framework for an optimal integration of different modes so as to enable an efficient and cost-effective use of the transport system through seamless, customer-orientated door-to-door services, while favouring competition between transport operators. Furthermore, the Community has adopted the promotion of intermodality[1] as a policy tool enabling a systems approach to transport.[2]

The provision and financing of transport infrastructure, as well as devising a system to charge for its use, have been two of the main stumbling blocks of the CTP. As early as the 1961 Memorandum, one of the two principal themes was the provision of infrastructure in the most economic and efficient way, and the means of paying for its use. In 1994 the European Council endorsed 14 Trans-European Networks-Transport (TENT)[3] projects of common interest as priorities. The fair allocation of infrastructure construction and upkeep costs is a major problem for the Community.

---

[1] 'Intermodality' or 'intermodal' transport is understood by the Commission as the movement of goods where at least two different modes are used in the door-to-door transport chain.

[2] COM (97) 243 final – Commission Communication entitled *Intermodality and Intermodal Freight Transport in the European Union.*

[3] Trans-European Networks are modern technologically advanced networks in the fields of transport, energy and telecommunications.

Combined transport

Current status

The first significant measure adopted in this field was Directive 75/130[4] setting out common rules for road/rail and road/inland waterways transportation of goods between member states, which was subsequently amended and consolidated by Directive 92/106.[5] Regulation 2196/98[6] lays down general rules for the granting of Community financial aid to promote combined transport.

Background

The efforts of the Community to develop combined transport have been principally directed to road/rail and road/inland waterways in order to make use of the over-capacity in the rail and inland waterway sectors. Combined transport has an economic advantage over long distance and helps to reduce road traffic with benefits for road safety, reduction of traffic congestion and protection of the environment.

Directive 75/130 promoted the development of road/rail and road/inland waterway combined transport. Directive 75/130 freed the road parts of the operation from quantitative restrictions and eliminated various administrative restraints. Member states were required to liberalize combined road/rail carriage from all quotas and authorization systems.[7] The Directive was amended a number of times to extend its scope to include the transport of units by inland waterways between member states, including feeder and final delivery transport by road; the reimbursement of national road tax on vehicles used in combined transport; own-account combined transport operations and the abolition of compulsory tariffs on feeder and final delivery road haulage legs.[8]

Common rules (Directive 92/106)

Since July 1993 the initial and final leg of a combined transport operation involving rail, inland waterways and also maritime services have been

---

4   OJ 1975 L 48/31.
5   OJ 1992 L 368/38.
6   OJ 1998 L 277/1.
7   This was not always willingly done. See e.g. Case C-45/89 *Commission v Italy* [1991] ECR I-2053.
8   The use of containers is particularly significant in combined transport so Recommendation 79/487, OJ 1979 L 125/18, was adopted on the ratification of the International Convention on Safe Containers (CSC).

freed from all quotas and authorization systems (Art. 2). The road sections are subject to the same limits as those applied to road haulage linked to inland waterway transport. 'Combined transport' is defined in the Directive as the transport of goods between member states where the lorry, trailer, semi-trailer, with or without tractor unit, swap body[9] or container of 20 feet or more, uses the road on the initial or final leg of the journey and, on the other leg, rail or inland waterway or maritime services where this section exceeds 100 km as the crow flies. In addition, the initial or final road transport leg of the journey must be made either between the point where the goods are loaded and the nearest suitable rail loading station for the initial leg, and between the nearest suitable rail unloading station and the point where the goods are unloaded for the final leg, or, within a radius not exceeding 150 km as the crow flies from the inland waterway port or seaport of loading or unloading (Art. 1(1)).

Directive 92/106 obliges member states to take measures necessary to ensure that the taxes listed in the Directive which are applicable to road vehicles (lorries, tractors, trailers or semi-trailers) when routed in combined transport, are reduced or reimbursed either by a standard amount or in proportion to the journeys that such vehicles undertake by rail, within limits and in accordance with conditions and rules they fix after consultation with the Commission (Art. 6). However, a Commission report on the application of the Directive between 1993 and 1995[10] concluded that the tax provisions had not been used in most member states and therefore had little practical effect on the development of combined transport. They are too limited, as they apply only to the rail transport of certain vehicles. Also the provisions concerning initial and final delivery transport have lost some of their competitive advantage since the liberalization of road haulage cabotage from July 1998. Thus it is proposed to amend the Directive to provide a more precise definition of combined transport, to add certain measures (particularly fiscal) to encourage combined transport and to lift the weekend, night, holiday period, etc. driving restrictions for initial and final road haulage.[11]

Financial assistance for infrastructure (Regulation 2196/98)

The Regulation provides financial assistance for innovative operational measures (and for feasibility studies which plan and prepare such meas-

---

[9] This refers to the part of a road vehicle on which it is intended that the load is to be placed and which may be detached from the vehicle and reincorporated therein.

[10] COM (97) 372 final.

[11] COM (98) 414 final.

ures) to promote combined transport actions until the end of 2001.[12] These actions are covered by the 1996 Guidelines for the development of TENT discussed below but it is also envisaged that the action may also cover routes situated partly outside Community territory (Arts 2 and 3).

Projects may be submitted by any member state or any private natural or legal person established in the Community (Art. 4(1)) but financial assistance is limited to 30% for innovative operational measures and to 50% for feasibility studies (Art. 5).

Intermodality

Intermodality is a characteristic of a transport system that allows at least two different modes to be used in an integrated manner in a door-to-door transport chain.[13] It goes beyond the Community's definition of combined transport since the only types of combined transport which limit road use in specified ways are promoted by the Community in secondary legislation adopted to promote combined transport.

Intermodality addresses the integration of modes of transport at three levels: infrastructure and transport means ('hardware'); operations and the use of infrastructure (especially terminals); and services and regulation. The policy is to eliminate a number of identified obstacles, such as lack of coherent network of modes and interconnections, lack of technical interoperability between and within modes, data-interchange and procedures.

The Commission has identified the key issues of intermodality as: a European strategy on infrastructure (TENT); a single transport market (harmonization of regulatory and competition rules); identification and elimination of obstacles to intermodality and the associated friction costs; and implementing the Information Society in the transport sector.

Infrastructure

Access to quality infrastructure which allows safe, swift, reliable and environmentally safe transport operations is essential for an integrated transport market to exist. Poor roads, congestion at airports, slow and inefficient railways result in inadequate services. Although most member states have devoted considerable resources to developing their transport

---

[12] In 1992 the Commission had launched an experimental five-year scheme for the granting of financial assistance for pilot schemes to promote combined transport – Decision 93/45, OJ 1993 L 16/55.
[13] See n. 2 above, p. 1.

infrastructure, these have inevitably been designed and constructed according to national needs and priorities at a time when their economies were far less dependent on each other. Thus Europe was faced with roads, railways, inland waterways, ports and airports infrastructures which did not function or relate to each other according to the needs of a Community-wide economy and society.

The Council could only agree as from 1990 on the adoption and implementation of Action Programmes providing for financial support for projects of Community interest in a number of priority modes of transport and routes.[14] However, the Treaty on European Union (TEU), which came into force in November 1993, added specific provisions to the EC Treaty which require the establishment and development of Trans-European Networks in specified areas including transport (Arts 154 to 156). These networks are to be achieved by a partnership between the Community and member states. Responsibility for creating transport networks lies mainly with the member states. The Community's role is to take project proposals from the member states and turn them into a network design, to encourage member states to take projects further and to try to find a way of overcoming financial and regulatory hindrances.

Provision and financing of general infrastructure

Inland transport (general)

Throughout the 1970s and 1980s, demand for transport was on the increase for both goods and passengers. Existing transport networks became afflicted by congestion (imposing huge costs on the European economy) and damaging of the environment. Furthermore, there were missing links between national infrastructures in the form of non-existent trans-border motorways, tunnels, railway lines and canals. Not all national networks were interoperable, making efficient, swift and safe travel across borders impossible. Railways were the prime example where power supplies, gauges, rolling stock specifications and many other technical matters forced changes of equipment at borders. As the Community enlarged, some regions and member states at the periphery lacked quality infrastructure compared with the central regions.

In 1976 two proposals were made. The first, Decision 78/174,[15] concerned the provision of a consultation procedure and the setting up of a Transport Infrastructure Committee. The consultation procedure was to

---

[14] Regulation 3359/90, OJ 1990 L 326/1.
[15] OJ 1978 L 54/16, repealed by Decision 1692/96, OJ 1996 L 228/1.

enable member states to take their planning decisions on infrastructure investment in accordance with Community criteria, thus avoiding violation of the interests of the national transport systems. The task of the Committee is to look at national infrastructure development programmes as an entity and eliminate bottlenecks in the planning and construction of a network of major trunk roads, railways and inland waterways. The Committee has carried out several studies and has done useful work in coordinating each member state's investment where this is of concern to other member states.

The second proposal took a long time to be adopted. Regulation 3359/90[16] provided support for projects with a Community interest. The goal of achieving an integrated market by 1992 resulted in this Regulation being adopted on an Action Programme to provide the infrastructure necessary to deal with the rising transport demand and to exploit fully the opportunities presented by the Single European Market. Meanwhile, Regulations had been adopted on the granting of limited financial support to projects of Community interests from the Community's budget.[17] For example, Regulation 4048/88[18] granted financial support to 12 transport infrastructure projects in order to use appropriations in the 1988 Community budget as well as those available in the 1989 budget. The support scheme worked as follows: where a particular project was declared to be of European impact, it became eligible for support from Community funds. The aid did not normally exceed 24% of the total cost or 50% for preparatory studies, except where other Community instruments provided for a higher level of contribution.

In June 1992 the Commission published its strategy for a Community transport infrastructure and approved a Communication on the method for infrastructure funding.[19] The Commission gave priority to establishing a combined transport system which builds up an effective railway network and which would permit state aids for projects promoting combined transport.

Railway infrastructure

Very little was done until the 1990s in respect of railway infrastructure and any developments in this sector were due mainly to the activities of the

---

[16] See n. 14.
[17] Regulations: 3600/82, OJ 1982 L 376/10; 1889/84, OJ 1984 L 177/4; 3620/84, OJ 1984 L 333/58; 4059/86, OJ 1986 L 378/24; 4070/87, OJ 1987 L 380/33; 4048/88, OJ 1988 L 356/5.
[18] *Ibid.*
[19] COM (92) 231 final.

International Union of Railways (IUR). Rail infrastructure, however, played a central role in the Community's 1990 Action Programme for completing an integrated transport market by 1992.[20]

Two Commission Communications are particularly relevant to railways as they enable infrastructure managers responsible for the operation of Freeways to identify potential routes and put the concept into practice. The first Communication, entitled *Trans European Rail Freight Freeways*,[21] explains the framework regulation and technical specifications which railway undertakings have to respect if they intend to set up Rail Freight Freeways as recommended by the Commission in its policy to revitalize rail transport.[22] The Communication sets out the criterion that the Freeways will have to be compatible with European legislation, especially with the competition rules. The concept of trans-European Rail Freight Freeways provides for the Freeways to be run by infrastructure managers from the national railway undertakings through a 'One-Stop Shop'. The infrastructure managers will identify and allocate capacity on the relevant Freeway. Thus the carrier will no longer have to contact the railway undertakings or authorities responsible in each member state it crosses. The managers will also monitor and control performance, establish the charging system and deal with complaints. The coordination of Freeways with TENT-rail and combination transport networks allows, where appropriate, that Freeways benefit from infrastructure improvements in the framework of projects of common interest.

The second Communication, entitled *Intermodality and Intermodel Freight transport in the European Union*,[23] sets out strategies and actions to enhance efficiency, services and sustainability.

Maritime structures

As far as maritime infrastructure is concerned, the Commission published at the end of 1997 two related documents: a Green Paper on *Ports and Maritime Infrastructures*[24] and a proposal emphasizing the need to integrate ports and other interconnections fully into the 1996 Revised TENT guidelines.[25] The Green Paper encourages various ways of improving port

---

[20] See n. 14 above.
[21] COM (97) 242 final.
[22] White Paper entitled *A Strategy for Revitalisation of the Community's Railways*, COM (96) 421 final, referred to in Chapter 3.
[23] See n. 2.
[24] COM (97) 678.
[25] COM (99) 277 final, amending Decision 1692/96 (discussed below) as regards seaports, inland ports and intermodal terminals.

infrastructure, increasing the efficiency of ports and their integration into the Community's transport network. The proposal is intended to bring 300 European ports into the TENT, giving priority to the funding of projects for short-sea shipping and combined transport involving railways. Corridors are to be created by upgrading existing road and rail links and by improving sea connections and ports giving access to Asia and North Africa. The initial link with Central and Eastern Europe is based on a network of ten corridors along the main trading routes. The corridors programme will encourage efficient multi-modal transport using rail for long-haul and road for shorter journeys.

Airports

The major concern as far as airports are concerned is to develop a single air traffic management system for Europe (ATM) and to prepare the sector for a global navigation system (GNSS). The Community also seeks to promote the enhancement of airport capacity as part of TENT.[26] Regional policy instruments may also be used to improve airports in peripheral regions.

ATM

The major issue for air transport in the field of technical harmonization is centred on air traffic management (ATM). As stated above the Commission has sought for a long time to set in place a European air traffic management system.

Meanwhile, two Directives have been adopted in order to incorporate into Community law the technical specification adopted by the European Organization for the Safety of Air Navigation (Eurocontrol). Directive 93/65[27] was adopted on the definition and use of compatible technical specifications for the procurement of air traffic management equipment and systems (e.g. communication, surveillance and navigation systems). The Directive requires the member states to ensure that the awarding civil entities refer to mandatory Eurocontrol specifications when purchasing ATM equipment and systems (Art. 5). A later measure, Commission Directive 97/15,[28] adopts Eurocontrol standards and amends Directive 93/65.

---

[26] For example, the inclusion of the development at Berlin, Milan and Athens airports. The new airport at Milan (Malpensa 2000) was among the 14 priority TENT projects.

[27] OJ 1993 L 187/52.

[28] OJ 1997 L 95/16.

GNSS

As far as GNSS is concerned, the Community's strategy is to contribute to the development of a trans-European positioning and navigation network (Galileo), supported by terrestrial systems. The policy is underpinned by a specific Action Plan for developing GNSS taking into account the work of experts in the field. The European programme is multi-modal and multi-sectoral in scope: the resulting navigation/positioning services will be available to all potential users, notably in the air, maritime and land transport sectors. Full implementation of Galileo is expected over the period 2000–2008.[29] The system is to be developed as a public-private partnership and will involve cooperation with Russia and possibly Japan to enable European industry to compete with the US.

In 1998 an agreement was reached between the Community, ESA (European Space Agency) and Eurocontrol concerning a European contribution to the development of GNSS. The Commission represents the Community in monitoring the implementation of this agreement and coordinating common approaches towards its realization.

Trans-European Networks – Transport

Current status

Decision 1692/96[30] sets out the current revised guidelines for the development of the TENT by 2010 and is aimed at *all* transport infrastructures, thus replacing the former separate guidelines for roads, inland waterways, the TGV and combined transport.[31] The guidelines cover the objectives, priorities and broad lines of measures envisaged in the sphere of trans-European networks and identifies projects of common interest. Regulation 2236/95[32] lays down the general rules for the granting of Community financial aid in the fields of trans-European networks.

Background

The TEU contains provisions requiring the Community to issue guidelines setting out the objectives, the priorities and broad lines of measures envis-

---

[29] COM (99) 54 final.
[30] OJ 1996 L 228/1.
[31] These earlier guidelines expired in 1995. COM(94)106. An Action Programme for 1995–2000 was then adopted, COM (95) 302.
[32] OJ 1995 L 228/1, amended by Regulation 1655/99, OJ 1999 L 197/1.

aged for the transport networks and to provide financial support for feasibility studies, loan guarantees or interest rates subsidies. Member states are required to plan their own national infrastructure with reference to the Community.

The importance of TENT is well recognized by the Community as one of the major ways of supporting growth and an essential component of the single market. Fourteen specific projects were identified in Annex III of the Community Guidelines (Decision 1692/96). The first report on the implementation of TENT shows significant progress.[33] However, the main obstacle is not in planning the infrastructure but in financing its construction.

Although the Community has assisted the financing of priority projects, new means of investment have to be found if the network is to be completed on schedule by 2010. In 1996 the Commission set up a High-Level Group to examine the role of public-private partnerships (PPPs) in accelerating the implementation of TENT. The recommendations of the High-Level Group were fully endorsed by the Commission in its 1997 Communication entitled *Public-Private Partnerships in Trans-European Transport Network Projects*.[34]

The Commission supported the creation of dedicated undertakings for the ownership, construction or financing of particular railway projects in order to facilitate the participation of the private sector in the investment effort. Thus the Commission launched a study at the end of 1997 on the possibility of creating risk-capital funds, financed in part from the Community budget. The aim of these funds are to provide a catalyst to encourage the large private sector institutions, such as the pension funds, to invest in TENT projects.

Also in 1997 the Commission issued a Communication setting out a pan-European dimension of transport policy including a proposal to link the Community's transport infrastructure networks to its neighbours.[35] The policy is aimed at sustainable, environmentally sound and efficient transport systems which not only address the social and economic disparities between the regions but also enhance Europe's competitiveness. The policy promotes economic and social cohesion in Europe.

---

[33] COM (98) 356 final.
[34] COM (97) 453 final.
[35] COM (97) 172 final entitled *Towards a Cooperative, Pan-European Transport Network*.

The revised guidelines (Decision 1692/96)

The Decision brings together, in a single framework, the outline plans for the road, railway, inland waterway, combined transport, port and airport networks. Thus, the master plan for TENT is based on a combination of all modes of transport, unlike the earlier guidelines, which were based on single modes of transport. It also covers traffic management and traffic control systems which have a direct impact on the efficiency and safety of the transport system as a whole. The guidelines will be adapted every five years in order to take account of economic and technological developments in the transport field (Art. 21).

The guidelines provide a general reference framework to identify projects of common interest permitting gradual integration of the networks at European level (Art. 7). The member states will then determine the details of projects, their routes, financing and the speed of implementation in accordance with national planning rules, in respect of the subsidiarity principle.

The projects identified with the assistance of the guidelines as being of common interest will be eligible for Community financial support through the budget heading for Trans-European networks or the Cohesion Fund. The conditions and procedures for granting such support have been laid down in specific measures.[36]

Trans-European Networks' financial regulation (Regulation 2236/95)

The main objective of this measure is to set down the general rules for granting Community financial assistance up to 2006 (as amended) in the field of trans-European Networks, which includes TENT. It covers all modes of transport including traffic management and interoperability. The financial assistance is not granted for the actual construction of networks (which is the responsibility of the member states and private investors) but for the launching or the acceleration of projects of common interest.

Financial assistance will be granted according to the degree of contribution to the objectives set out in Art. 154 of the Treaty, that is, interconnection and interoperability of national networks, access to these networks, need to link island, landlocked and peripheral regions – and to other objectives and priorities defined in the 1996 guidelines.[37]

.

---

[36] Regulation 1164/94, OJ 1994 L 130/1, establishing the Cohesion Fund and Regulation 2236/95, OJ 1995 L 228/1, laying down general rules for granting Community financial aid in the field of trans-European networks, including transport.

[37] In implementing the Regulation the Commission is assisted in the usual manner by a committee comprising representatives of the member states.

A number of matters should be taken into account in taking a decision. These are: the maturity of the project; the stimulative effect on public and private finance; the soundness of the financial package; direct or indirect socio-economic effects, in particular on employment; and the environmental consequence. In cross border projects the synchronization of the construction of different parts of the project should also be taken into consideration.

Member states and other bodies, including the private sector with the consent of the member state concerned, may submit applications for financial assistance. The Regulation provides for the following forms of finance: co-financing of studies (normally up to 50% of the total cost); subsidies of the interest of loans; contributions towards fees for guarantees for loans; direct grants for investment in duly justified cases; and risk-capital form of funding (amended Art. 4). However, the Regulation provides that, irrespective of the form of the intervention chosen, the total amount of Community assistance to projects must not exceed 10% of the total investment cost except for projects concerning satellite positioning and navigation systems where the investment may reach 20% (amended Art. 5).

Railways

The arrival of the high-speed train (HST) highlighted the need for action and the Council responded by adopting Directive 96/48[38] on the interoperability of the trans-European high-speed rail system.

The Directive is concerned with projects for the construction, upgrading and operation of the infrastructures and rolling stock which will contribute to the functioning of the system. The Directive limits itself to those elements of the HST network that need to be compatible to ensure interoperability. It is not concerned with the specific design of the equipment but with interfaces. It identifies subsystems for the preparation of Technical Specifications for Interoperability (TSIs). Drafts of the TSI are prepared for the Commission by a joint representative body made up of the railways and the industry. If the Commission accepts the proposals they will then be forwarded to an expert Committee of the member states for an opinion. In the light of the opinion of this Committee, the Commission then adopts the TSIs, which will then be mandatory throughout the Community.

A further proposal has been published on the interoperability of trans-

---

[38] OJ 1996 L 235/6.

European conventional rail systems.[39] It sets out to establish the conditions to be met concerning the design, construction, putting into service, upgrading, renewal, operation and maintenance of the parts of this system put into service after the Directive comes into force.

Charging for use of infrastructure

Background

The more integrated the European market has become, the more urgent the need to find an agreed formula for charging for the use of the infrastructure. The debate on how to charge has been very controversial, as an efficient and fair pricing system must differentiate between types of vehicles and times and places of travel to reflect that costs do differ.

How to allocate costs for the damage done to the infrastructure by its users is a long-standing problem. Member states operate different charging systems (e.g. fuel tax, vehicle tax or tolls) which reflect national and historical preferences. These systems are inadequate to deal with the liberalization of international transport services. Furthermore, the balance between different modes of transport will not be achieved unless the significant differences in the way infrastructure and external costs (congestion, accidents, noise and pollution) are charged in various parts of the Community are eliminated. Differences in charging systems in different member states can also distort competition even within a single mode of transport, giving some national industries advantages over others.

Until the middle of the 1980s very few measures had been adopted with respect to the financial costs of transport infrastructure. Regulation 1108/70[40] introduced an accounting system for expenditure on infrastructure in respect of transport by rail, road and inland waterway (i.e. inland transport). The Regulation was implemented by Commission Regulation 2598/70,[41] which specified the items to be included under the various headings in the forms of accounts shown in Annex I of Regulation 1108/70. These measures were not, however, concerned with the daily costs of using the infrastructure.

---

[39] COM (99) 617 final.
[40] OJ 1970 L 130/4, regularly amended.
[41] OJ 1970 L 278/1.

Road transport

Current status

Directive 99/62[42] adjusts national charges for heavy goods vehicles using certain infrastructure. Member states must impose a charge on these vehicles at or above the minimum rate set in an Annex to the Directive.

Background

Much thought has been given to developing an equitable system of collecting motor vehicle taxation for heavy goods vehicles which would enable road hauliers to be charged reasonably for the upkeep of the road infrastructure. Several options have been considered. The first option was an annual tax imposed by the member state authorizing the vehicle on the road (the nationality principle). The second option was a tax on fuel, which would mean that the countries through which the lorries travelled would be more likely to recover some of the cost of maintaining the road infrastructure. The third option was a road toll (the territoriality principle).

In 1986, a Commission study on *Elimination of Distortions of Competition of a Fiscal Nature in the Transport of Goods by Road: Study of vehicle taxes, fuel taxes and road tolls* was published.[43] This resulted in a Commission Communication setting out the various options for a new system of taxation of commercial vehicles. Since 1989 the Commission favoured the argument that road hauliers should be charged in the member state where they use roads (the territoriality principle) as opposed to the member state where their vehicles are registered (the nationality principle). However, the territoriality principle will only work fairly if reliable statistics are provided from the authorities of the member states.[44]

In addition, the technical means had to be found to monitor the use of motorways used by heavy goods vehicles. In 1990 Germany, which supported the territoriality principle, decided to impose, in the absence of Community action, its own tax (tax stickers for 16 tonne vehicles travelling through Germany on motorways and federal roads). The Commission brought an action against Germany seeking a declaration that Germany had failed to fulfil its Treaty obligations; the Commission considered such a tax to be discriminatory against vehicles registered in other member

---

[42] OJ 1999 L 187/42.
[43] COM (86) 750.
[44] Regulation 1172/98, OJ 1998 L 163/1 on statistical returns in respect of the carriage of goods by road.

states, since German hauliers, who would also have to pay for the sticker, would benefit at the same time from reduced taxes. The ECJ confirmed the Commission's view.[45]

After a lengthy and controversial debate, Directive 93/89[46] introduced a common tax system, the Eurovignette, for haulage vehicles using Community roads. This Directive was annulled on procedural grounds by the European Court of Justice[47] but remained in force until the adoption of Directive 99/62.[48] The replacement measure took a long time to be adopted as the Commission decided to take the opportunity to revise the Eurovignette system and the interoperability of road-pricing systems in parallel with the wider discussions on the Green and White Papers on pricing for use of infrastructure.

At the end of 1995 the Commission published a Green Paper discussion document on pricing entitled *Towards Fair and Efficient Pricing in Transport*[49] to focus public debate on how the true costs of transport should be borne more fairly by those who generate them. A White Paper, *Fair Payment for Infrastructure Use: A phased approach to transport infrastructure charging in the European Union,*[50] followed in 1998 adopting the 'user pays' principle. This envisages a framework for the gradual harmonization (between 1998 and 2008) of transport infrastructure charging. The modification of the road and rail taxation system is based on two factors: the number of kilometres covered (monitored by means of tachographs and vehicle weight)[51] and marginal costs of access of, for example, one vehicle over a certain distance. Thus the user pays for the additional costs imposed on the system, like road infrastructure damage, but not unavoidable costs imposed on society by such use, for example congestion, accidents, noise and pollution.[52]

Charging of heavy goods vehicles (Directive 99/62)

The Directive harmonizes the national vehicle tax systems and establishes fair mechanisms for charging infrastructure costs to hauliers. The Directive applies only to commercial vehicles of more than 12 tonnes gross laden

45 Case C-195/90 *Commission v Germany* [1992] ECR I-3141.
46 OJ 1993 L 279/32.
47 Case C-21/94 *European Parliament v Council* [1995] ECR I-1827.
48 OJ 1999 L 187/42.
49 COM (95) 691 final.
50 COM (98) 466.
51 Europe No. 7268, 23 July 1998.
52 The proposals contrast with the ones for ports and airports which appear to prefer a greater degree of cost recovery.

weight (Art. 2). Vehicle taxes listed in the Directive shall be charged solely by the member state of registration (Arts 3 and 5). Minimum rates are set for the vehicles taxes applied by member states (Annex I). Provision is made for reduction in charges to be applied to less polluting and road-friendly vehicles. Temporary derogations are provided for some member states (Greece, Italy, Portugal and Spain) (Art. 6(1)) and for certain local domestic transport operations with little impact on the Community transport market (Art. 6(2)). Reduced rates or exemptions of vehicle taxes are also permitted in case of vehicles whose use is not liable to affect the Community transport market (Art. 6(3)). Procedures have been introduced to allow further exemptions or reductions for certain special situations.

As far as user charges are concerned, member states are allowed to charge for the use of bridges, tunnels and mountain passes (Art. 7(2)). However, such charges should not be discriminatory on the grounds of the nationality of the haulier or the origin or destination of the vehicle (Art. 7(4)) nor entail excessive formalities or create obstacles at internal borders (Art. 7(5)). The rates of charges should be based on the duration of the use made of the infrastructure in question and be differentiated in relation to costs caused by the road vehicles (Art. 7(8)). User charges shall be set by the member state concerned at a level which is not higher than the maximum rates laid down in Annex II (Art. 7(7)). Rules for determining user charges are laid down, such as the characteristics of the infrastructure to which they are applicable, the maximum levels of certain rates and other general conditions that will have to be complied with; weighted average tolls should be related to the costs of construction, operating and developing the infrastructure network concerned (Art. 7(9) and (10)).

Finally, member states are allowed to attribute to environmental protection and the balanced development of transport networks a percentage of the amount of the user charge or of the toll, provided that this amount is calculated in accordance with the provisions of the Directive (Art. 9(2)).

Rail transport[53]

As far as infrastructure fees are concerned there must be no discrimination in the charging for services of an equivalent nature in the same market and member states have to lay down rules for determining the fees. The fees charged by the infrastructure manager shall be fixed according to the nature of the service, the period of use, the market conditions and the type and degree of wear and tear on the infrastructure.[54]

---

[53] See Chapter 3, where relevant measures are discussed.
[54] Arts 7 and 8 of Directive 95/19, OJ 1995 L 143/75.

The adoption of an infrastructure package on costs and conditions for using rail is likely to be adopted before the end of 2000.[55] The measure will replace Directive 95/19 on the breakdown of infrastructure capacities and the levying of fees. The proposal will set up a method for calculating fees on the basis of costs directly linked to rail transport by taking into consideration the problems caused by scarcity of capacity. Furthermore, prior publication of pricing systems will be made compulsory.

Maritime transport

The Green Paper on ports and maritime infrastructure,[56] which has already been mentioned, proposes that whoever uses the port infrastructure should bear the real cost of port services and facilities. The ownership, organization and administration of ports varies greatly between member states. The Commission, however, intends to introduce a principle of recovering the cost of new investments, operating and external costs to ensure that the new investments are demand-driven and to ensure fair competition between ports.

Air transport

The amended proposed Directive on airport charges[57] does not intend to harmonize charges but to establish uniform criteria based on the principles of non-discrimination, 'cost-relatedness' and transparency of charges. It applies to any Community airport open to commercial traffic. The application of these principles needs to take several factors into account when applied, such as capacity problems at certain airports or environmental concerns.

The proposed criteria would seek to ensure that charging systems would not discriminate between domestic and intra-Community air services and that the level of airport charges would be set in a reasonable relation to the actual cost of the facilities and the services provided. The debate focuses on the use of charges to cross-subsidize smaller regional airports and on the variability of charges to reflect environmental conditions. The Commission admits that the principle of cost-relatedness does not exclude the functioning of such a system under certain conditions. Finally, the proposal introduces minimum requirements to inform users (transparency). The proposal is linked to another proposal for a directive on access to

---

[55] See Chapter 3.
[56] COM (97) 678, Chapter 4.
[57] COM (98) 509 final.

ground handling market.[58] The intention is to build on the liberalization of the European aviation market which was achieved by the third civil aviation package.

Concluding observations

The provision and financing of transport infrastructure, as well as devising an acceptable scheme to raise funds to maintain the infrastructure, has been a difficult problem to resolve. Without doubt the TENT concept has given impetus and a legal framework to move forward. The problems of raising of capital to provide and maintain the infrastructure have been resolved under the public-private partnerships and the agreed 'user pays' principle.

---

[58] See Chapter 7.

Competition rules and external relations

Introduction

In this chapter a brief overview will be given of the EC Competition Rules (Arts 81 and 82) and the state aid rules (Arts 87 and 88), identifying the legislative measures adopted specifically to implement the rules in the transport sector.[1] The international nature of transport services has enabled the Community to extend its competence (although normally shared with the member states) in concluding agreements concerning transport matters with non-Community countries.[2]

The EC Competition Rules

General background

The Competition Rules apply to all economic sectors including transport.[3] Article 81 prohibits agreements, decisions or concerted practices between undertakings which have the object or effect of preventing, restricting or distorting competition and affecting trade between member states. Thus in the context of agreements between transport undertakings, whether between various branches of transport or between different undertakings in the same branch of transport, if such agreements restrict competition, they are *prima facie* prohibited under Art. 81(1). Yet these types of agreements are, in general, favourably regarded by the transport policies of the member states.

An agreement which infringes Art. 81 is automatically void under Art. 81(2). However, if the conditions of Art. 81(3) are fulfilled, an exemption from the application of Art. 81(1) can be granted by the Commission. Article 81(3) enables some agreements which restrict competition to be

---

[1] See Further Reading.
[2] But see Opinion 1/94, [1994] ECR I-5267.
[3] Case 156/77 *Commission v Belgium* [1978] ECR 1881.

exempted if the agreement also contains positive elements which will bene-fit the consumer. Article 82, which complements Art. 81, prohibits any abuse by an undertaking of a dominant position within the common mar-ket or in a substantial part of it insofar as it may affect trade between member states.

The competition rules do not, however, provide a comprehensive proce-dure for their application. Nevertheless, Art. 83(1) empowers the Council, on a proposal from the Commission, to adopt the necessary measures to implement the rules, which it has done by enacting Regulation 17.[4] The Regulation grants powers to the Commission to initiate and carry out investigations to determine whether certain practices are anti-competitive. The Regulation also lays down procedural rules and safeguards for those undertakings being subjected to an investigation. However, Regulation 141/62[5] (extended by Regulation 1002/67[6]) was adopted suspending the application of Regulation 17 to the transport industry until the adoption of Regulation 1017/68,[7] which applied the competition rules to inland transport. Even then, shipping and air transport were indefinitely excluded from the scope of the Regulation. Specific regulations have now been enacted applying the competition rules to sea and air transport, and these are discussed below.

As far as procedural rules are concerned, Commission Regulations 2842/98 and 2843/98[8] are the most recent relevant measures. The first Regu-lation, on the hearing of parties during investigations, applies to all anti-competitive practices including those in the transport sector. The second Regulation, on the form, content, etc. of applications and notifi-cations, only concerns the transport sector but applies to all modes of transport.

Since the adoption of legislation applying Arts 81 and 82 to the trans-port sector, particularly to the 'protected' maritime and air modes, there have been a significant number of Commission investigations and ECJ rul-ings which have had major impact in the interpretation and application of the EC Treaty provisions themselves.[9]

---

4 OJ Sp Ed 1962, No. 204/62, p. 87.
5 OJ 1962 p. 2751.
6 JO 1967 No. 306/1.
7 JO 1967 L 175/1, supplemented by Regulations 1629/69 OJ 1969 L 209/1; 1630/69 OJ 1969 L 209/11; 2988/74 OJ 1974 L 319/1.
8 OJ 1998 L 354/18 and L 354/22.
9 See books on EC Competition Law in Further Reading and, e.g: Case C-179/90, *Porto di Genova* [1991] ECR I-5889; *Sea Containers/Stena Sealink* [1995] 5 CMLR 84; *Port of Rodby* OJ 1994 L 55/52; *Port of Roscoff* [1995] CMLR 177; and *Port of Elsinor* [1996] 4 CMLR 728.

As far as mergers are concerned, the relevant general measure is Regulation 4064/89.[10]

Inland transport

The basic measure (Regulation 1017/68)

Having excluded the application of Regulation 17, and in view of the special characteristics of the transport industry, the Council thought it necessary to adopt specific rules for the implementation of the EC competition rules. Thus Regulation 1017/68[11] was enacted in order to bring the three inland modes of transport within the scope of the rules without discouraging agreements of possible benefit to the users of transport services in such areas as improved technology and standardization.

The Regulation applies to all modes of inland transport but it had little effect on the railway sector since most railway systems at the time were state-owned. The Regulation closely follows the provisions of Regulation 17. It generally prohibits agreements, decisions and concerted practices which prevent, restrict or distort competition in the common market (Art. 2). Agreements between small and medium-sized undertakings are exempted where they are designed to consolidate such undertakings into groupings as long as they remain within specific capacity limits (Art. 4). The Regulation also applies for exemption for technical cooperation agreements. Furthermore, agreements concerned with improvement of transport services may also be exempt (Art. 12). Another feature of the Regulation is that it gives special consideration to agreements that may serve to mitigate disturbances in the transport industry (Art. 6).

As far as abuse of a dominant position is concerned, the Regulation closely follows Art. 82, citing four instances in which an undertaking or group of undertakings may be abusing a dominant position (Art. 8). The Regulation grants to the Commission the normal powers and duties as granted by Regulation 17.

Maritime transport

The first major hurdle the Community had to overcome as far as maritime transport was concerned was how to respond to the United Nations Code on Liner Conferences,[12] since several member states wished to ratify the

---

[10] OJ 1989 L 395/1, as amended by Regulation 1310/97, OJ 1997 L 180/1.

[11] See n. 7 above.

[12] Liner conference is a group of carriers of cargo on a particular route within geographical limits, and which have an agreement within the framework of which they operate under uniform or common freight rates and any other agreed conditions with respect to the provisions of liner services.

Code and fulfil their international obligations. This was achieved by adopting Community legislation to lay down rules for the operation of the Code by the member states.[13] However, the major legislative measure laying down detailed rules for the application of Arts 81 and 82 was Regulation 4056/86.[14] Another measure adopted at the same time was Regulation 4057/86[15] on unfair pricing practices, which provided the legal basis for the Community to counteract such practices of shipping lines registered in non-Community countries.

The basic measure (Regulation 4056/86)

The Regulation provides for deregulation, legal certainty, furtherance of Community integration and clarification of the position of maritime transport users. It was designed with the aim of reaching a fair balance between shipowners and users.

The Regulation applies 'only to international maritime services from or to one or more Community ports ...' (Art. 1(2)). Thus any agreement which covers maritime and land transport has to be investigated under two separate Regulations. The Regulation, however, is a hybrid instrument. It not only provides the means for applying the EC competition rules to maritime transport but also provides exceptions, block exemptions[16] and procedural rules for applying for individual exemptions under Art. 81(3). An exception is provided for certain technical agreements (Art. 2) and a block exemption is granted for agreements between transport users themselves or between users and conferences concerning rates, conditions and quality of liner services (Art. 6). Furthermore, the Regulation contains another block exemption for liner conference agreements. The Regulation sets out detailed provisions as to when the liner conferences themselves may be exempt *en bloc* from the prohibition of Art. 81(1) (Art. 5). As the block exemption is only available to liner conferences, Commission Regulation 870/95[17] had to be adopted in order to exempt other types of maritime arrangements such as consortia.

As far as abuse of a dominant position is concerned, Art. 8 confirms the direct effect of Art. 82 and its automatic application without the need for a

---

[13] Regulation 954/79. See Chapter 4.

[14] OJ 1986 L 378/4.

[15] OJ 1986 L 378/14. The Regulation is modelled on the Community's anti-dumping legislation.

[16] Block exemption regulations permit agreements, which comply precisely with specified conditions and obligations to be exempt from the prohibition of Art. 81(1) without the parties having to apply to the Commission for an individual exemption.

[17] OJ 1995 L 89/7.

prior decision.[18] Where the conduct of an exempted liner conference has effects incompatible with Art. 82, the Commission *may* withdraw the benefit of the automatic exemption, but before taking the decision the Commission *may* address to the conference recommendations for termination of the infringement.

Air transport

As part of the 1987 civil aviation package, Regulation 3975/87[19] was adopted laying down the procedure for the application of Arts 81 and 82 to air transport and Regulation 3976/87[20] provides for block exemptions for certain categories of agreements (subject to strict conditions).

Regulation 3975/87 follows a similar pattern to those enacted for the other modes of transport and, in particular, the inland transport Regulation. The Regulation applies only to *air transport* and not to ancillary services, which fall under the general regulation, Regulation 17.

Regulation 3976/87 empowers the Commission to apply Art. 81(3) of the EC Treaty by Regulation to certain categories of agreements (e.g. joint planning and coordination of airline schedules and consultation on tariffs for the carriage of passengers and baggage) which fall within the scope of Art. 83(1). The most recent measure is Commission Regulation 1083/93,[21] which extends block exemptions for certain categories of agreements until July 2001.

Other important measures which concern air transport include Regulation 2299/89[22] and Directive 96/67[23] on access to the ground-handling market at Community airports.

State aids

As stated in Chapter 2, the Treaty provisions on state aids apply to the transport industry but Art. 73 contains additional exceptions. The objective of Art. 73 is to ensure that national measures adopted to coordinate transport, and any aids that may be granted together with such measures, are compatible with the CTP and allow for conditions of competition. Thus the Article applies only to aids in the scope of Art. 87(1), namely government subsidies to transport undertakings.

---

[18] See e.g. Cases T-24-6 and 28/93 *Compagnie Maritime Belge Transports SA v Commission* [1997] 4 CMLR 273.
[19] OJ 1987 L 374/1.
[20] OJ 1987 L 374/9.
[21] OJ 1999 L 131/27.
[22] OJ 1989 L 220/1.
[23] OJ 1996 L 272/36.

The basic EC Treaty provisions are to be found in Arts 87 to 89. Article 87 sets out the basic prohibition together with a number of mandatory and discretionary circumstances where such aids will be compatible with the common market. The Commission has exclusive competence to authorize a state aid where the aid can only be permitted under the discretionary condition (Art. 87(3)). Article 88 is concerned with enforcement. The Article requires the Commission to monitor state aids (Art. 88(1)), imposes a duty on member states to notify state aids to the Commission before granting them (Art. 88(3)) and provides for a Commission investigative procedure to be undertaken under Art. 88(2).

Inland transport

The measures of general application adopted are: Council Decision 65/271,[24] laying down a legislative programme; Regulation 1191/69,[25] defining the concept of public service in inland transport (see Chapter 3); and Regulation 1107/70,[26] defining appropriate procedures for permissible aids as provided by Art. 73.

Maritime transport

As far as this mode of transport is concerned, the Community has adopted a series of directives in order to assist the ship-building industry. The policy on ship-building is embodied in Directive 87/167,[27] the sixth Directive on aid to ship-building.

Air transport

The liberalization of this transport sector, together with the privatization of the state-owned airlines, resulted in a near crisis in the early 1990s. As airlines sought financial assistance from their national governments, the Commission had to consider a number of notifications seeking exemption from the prohibition of Art. 88(1) on the granting of state aid. The Commission decisions and the rulings from the ECJ on state aids to airlines have contributed much to the body of general law that now governs the interpretation and application of Arts 87 and 88.[28]

---

[24] JO 1965 No. 88, p. 1500.
[25] OJ 1969 L 156/1.
[26] OJ 1970 L 130/1, frequently amended.
[27] OJ 1987 L 69/55.
[28] See Greaves, 'Judicial Review of Commission State Aid Decisions in Air Transport', ch. 39 in *Liber Amicorum for Gordon Slynn* (2000).

External competence

One of the distinctive features of the transport industry is its international nature, particularly so in respect of maritime and air transport. Although international transport services were historically regulated by bilateral and multilateral agreements (ensuring access and unhindered transit through states), measures adopted to liberalize this industry within the Community have replaced the bilateral agreements between member states. However, the EC Treaty is silent on matters relating to the external relations of this industry. Thus transport services between member states and third countries remain largely bilateral, even though in some modes of transport the Community has replaced the member states and negotiates on behalf of the Community.

As far as existing international obligations are concerned, Art. 307 restates the general principle of international law that the EC Treaty does not affect previous contractual obligations of the member states with third countries. However, as between themselves, member states cannot rely on this Treaty provision to assert rights under prior international agreements which are inconsistent with the obligations under the EC Treaty.[29] Furthermore, the member states have a duty, under Art. 307, para. 2, to take 'all appropriate steps to eliminate any incompatibilities' in existing agreements with non-member states.[30] Member states also have an obligation not to conclude treaties inconsistent with the EC Treaty.

As far as the Commission is concerned, the Community promotes cooperation with its neighbours.[31]

Inland transport

As far as road transport is concerned, external *exclusive* competence in inland transport matters was established early. Transit between member states via third countries had to be secured. The European Court ruled in *Re the European Road Transport Agreement: EC Commission v EC Council* ('the *ERTA* case')[32] that the Community had implied external competence where it was necessary to negotiate with third countries in order to achieve an objective of the EC Treaty.

---

[29] Case 10/61 *Commission v Italy* [1962] ECR 1.
[30] Case 12/79 *Attorney General v Burgoa* [1980] ECR 2787 and Case 181/80 *Procureur-General v Arbelaiz-Emazabel* [1981] ECR 2961.
[31] See e.g. COM (97) 172 final, entitled *Connecting the Union's transport infrastructure network to its neighbours*.
[32] Case 22/70 [1971] ECR 263.

The facts of the case were as follows: an agreement concerning the work of the crew of vehicles engaged in international transport had been signed in 1962 but negotiations for its revision were initiated in 1967 under the supervision of the UN Economic Commission for Europe. At the same time the Community itself adopted a legislative measure harmonizing the driving and rest periods of drivers of road transport vehicles.[33] The Council discussed the negotiations at a meeting in 1979 and agreed on a common view to be adopted by the member states at a forthcoming meeting. The negotiations were concluded by the member states according to what had been agreed at the Council's meeting. The Commission, however, objected to the manner in which the agreement had been reached and sought an annulment of the Council's discussions. The European Court of Justice ruled that the Community had competence to conclude international agreements in this field. As the Community had adopted measures on the same subject matter as the one being negotiated at international level (i.e. the Community had occupied the field), the *exclusive* authority to negotiate and conclude agreements belonged to the Community from the moment the Community measures had been adopted.

However, the facts of this particular case were such that the Court had no difficulty in declaring that, since the negotiations had been carried out before the Community had adopted the internal measure, the Council had been correct in proceeding in the manner they had done. The negotiations were at a critical stage, where it would have been unwise to have informed the non-Community countries that there had been a new distribution of powers within the Community.

As far as inland transport is concerned, the most important negotiations have been those with Switzerland. Swiss laws impose restrictions on the weight of heavy goods vehicles and prohibition on night traffic of such vehicles. In 1995 the mandate was widened to include air transport matters based on the Third Civil Aviation Package (excluding cabotage) and agreement was reached.[34]

Similarly, negotiations with Romania, Hungary and Bulgaria to facilitate transit with Greece are currently being undertaken.

Maritime and air transport

As far as maritime and air transport are concerned, the member states have been very reluctant to transfer competence of any sort to the Community.

---

[33] Regulation 543/69 OJ 1969 L 77/49.
[34] COM (99) 229 final.

For example, the Commission has failed to persuade the member states to let it represent them in international bodies such the International Maritime Organisation (IMO) when revising existing Conventions such as the 1968 Convention on Standards of Training, Certification and Watchkeeping (STCW).

Nevertheless, the Council often gives mandates to the Commission to negotiate on behalf of the Community and the member states, but once the agreement is ready for signature they are unwilling to give up their right to conclude the Treaty. Nevertheless, in March 1995, the Council requested that the Commission submit a Communication on external relations which would define general guidelines on the issues to be given priority in relations between the Community and non-Community countries and on action to be taken within international bodies. Furthermore, in 1998, the Council adopted mandates authorizing the Commission to negotiate maritime agreements with India and China;[35] this was the first time member states have granted the Commission such a mandate.

The Commission, however, has found an effective solution for making internationally agreed rules binding in the Community's legal order. Once the agreement has been reached, the Commission proposes a Directive or a Regulation to implement the rules within the Community.

A similar picture emerges in matters concerning international air transport agreements. The Commission is keen to obtain exclusive competence to negotiate commercial air services agreements with third countries on behalf of the Community.[36] In 1990 the Commission published a Communication[37] claiming competence on the basis of the *ERTA* case. This was followed in 1992 with another Communication[38] which argued the case in a less aggressive manner. The Council responded by setting up a Council Aviation Group to advance discussion on external relations. Unfortunately, this was followed by a period of controversy over the 'open sky' bilateral agreements with the US entered into by several member states. The Commission no longer claimed *exclusive* competence but argued strongly that it would be more fruitful for the Community to negotiate with the US *en bloc* rather than for each member state to negotiate and sign a separate bilateral agreement. Community objectives would be safeguarded. The Council reacted by asking the Commission to submit a

---

[35] Bull. E.U. 1998 (1–2) 1.3.192–193.

[36] For an explanation of the legal obstacles to this claim see J. Goh, *European Air Transport Law and Competition* (1997), ch. 15.

[37] COM (90) 17 final, entitled *Community Relations with Third Countries in Aviation Matters.*

[38] COM (92) 434 final, entitled *Air Transport Relations with Third Countries.*

report defining the 'common interest' and explaining why and to what extent the Community's approach would be economically more advantageous than the 'open sky' bilateral agreements negotiated by the six member states.

In the past there have been special cases when the Community concluded air transport agreements with non-Community countries. For example, in 1992, such an agreement was concluded with Norway and Sweden:[39] the mandate was based on the first, second and third civil aviation packages (excluding cabotage).

Recently the Commission has also been authorized on behalf of the Community to open negotiations on the Community's membership of Eurocontrol.

---

[39] Council Decision 92/384, OJ 1992 L 200/20, as amended by Council Decision 93/453, OJ 1993 L 212/17.

TABLES OF KEY
LEGISLATIVE MEASURES

Table 1: Access to the market – key legislation

	LICENCES	TARIFFS	CONTROLS	CABOTAGE	ACCESS TO OCCUPATION
ROAD	Dr 84/647, L335/72 Reg 881/92, L95/1 Reg 684/92, L74/1 Reg 11/98, L4/1 Reg 2121/98, L268/10	Reg 11, 1960, p.1121 Reg 1191/69, L156/1 Reg 4058/89 L390/1	Reg 4060/89, L390/18 Reg 3912/92, L395/6	Reg 3118/93, L279/1 Reg 12/98, L4/10	Dr 96/26, L124/1 Dr 98/76, L277/17
RAIL	Dr 91/440, L237/25 Dr 95/18, L143/70 Dr 95/19, L143/75	Reg 11, 1960, p.1121 Reg 1191/69 L156/1 Reg 2183/78, L258/1 Dec 82/529, L234/5 Dec 83/418, L237/32			
INLAND WATERWAYS	Dr 76/135, L21/10 Dr 82/714, L301/1 Reg 2919/85, L280/4 Reg 1356/96, L175/7 Reg 718/99, L90/1 Reg 2407/92, L240/1	Reg 11, 1960, p.1121 Reg 1191/69, L156/1 Dr 96/75, L304/12	Reg 4060/89, L390/18	Reg 3921/91, L373/1	Dr 87/540, L322/20
PROVISION OF SERVICES					
MARITIME	Reg 954/79, L121/1 Reg 4055/86, L378/1 Reg 4058/86, L378/21	Reg 4056/86, L378/4		Reg 3577/92, L364/7	Reg 613/91, L68/1
AIR	Reg 2408/92, L240/8 Reg 95/93, L14/1	Reg 2409/92, L240/15		Reg 2408/92, L240/8	Reg 2407/92, L240/1

Table 2: Harmonization – key legislation

	SOCIAL	SAFETY	ENVIRONMENT	TECHNICAL
ROAD	Reg 3820/85, L370/1 Reg 3821/85, L370/8 Reg 2135/98, L274/1 Dr 88/599, L325/55	Dr 72/166, L103/1 Dr 76/914, L357/36 Dr 91/439, L237/16 Dr 92/6, L57/27 Dr 92/24, L129/154 Dr 94/55, L319/7 Dr 95/50, L249/35 Dr 96/35, L145/10 Dr 96/96, L46/1	Dr 70/220, L76/1 Dr 70/157, L42/1 Dr 88/77, L36/33	Dr 70/156, L42/1 Dr 96/53, L235/59 Dr 98/91, L11/25
RAIL		Dr 95/19, L143/75 Dr 96/35, L145/10 Dr 96/49, L235/25		Dr 96/48, L235/6
INLAND WATERWAYS	Reg 718/99, L90/1	Dr 82/714, L301/1 Dr 91/672, L373/29 Dr 96/35, L145/10 Dr 96/50, L235/31		Dr 76/135, L21/10 Dr 82/714, L301/1
MARITIME	Dr 92/29, L113/19 Dr 95/21, L157/1 Dr 99/63, L167/33 Dr 99/95, L14/29	Dr 79/115, L33/32 Dr 93/75, L247/19 Dr 94/57, L319/20 Dr 94/58, L319/28 Dr 95/21, L157/1 Reg 3051/95, L320/14 Dr 97/70, L34/1 Dr 98/18, L144/1 Dr 98/41, L188/35	Dr 79/116, L33/33 Dr 2978/94, L319/1	Dr 96/98, L46/25
AIR		Dr 91/670, L373/21 Reg 3922/91, L373/4 Dr 94/56, L319/14	Dr 80/51, L18/16 Dr 89/629, L363/27 Dr 92/14, L76/21 Reg 925/99, L115/1	Dr 93/65, L187/52 Dr 97/15, L95/16

BIBLIOGRAPHY

Books

Abbati, C., (1987) *Transport and European Integration*, EEC Perspectives (Commission of the EC, Luxembourg)

Bathurst, M. E., K. R. Simmonds, N. M. Hunnings and J. Welch, (1972) 'Transport and the EEC: Great Britain and the Republic of Ireland' in *Legal Problems of an Enlarged Community*, Part IV on transport (Stevens, London)

Bredima-Savopoulou, A. and J. Tzoanos, (1990) *The Common Shipping Policy of the EC* (North-Holland, Amsterdam)

De Coninck, F., (1992) *European Air Law: New Skies for Europe* (Les Presses, Paris)

Despicht, N., (1964) *Policies for Transport in the Common Market* (Lambarde Press, Sidcup)

— (1969) *The Transport Policy of the European Communities* (Policy Studies Institute, London)

Erdmenger, J., (1983) *The European Community Transport Policy: Towards a CTP* (Gower, London)

Goh, J., (1997) *European Air transport Law and Competition* (Wiley, Chichester)

Greaves, R., (1991) *Transport Law of the European Community* (Athlone, London)

Power, V., (1992) *EC Shipping Law* (Lloyd's, London)

Schmit, P. H. and P. Herzog, (1976) *A Commentary on the EEC Treaty II* (Bender, New York)

Vaughan, D. (ed.), (1986) *Law of the European Communities* Vol. 2 (Butterworths, London)

Reports

Dawson, R. and G. Renaux, (1989) *EEC Transport Policy* (Clube de Bruxelles)

Trans, D. G., (1999) *Guide to the transport Acquis* (Brussels)

Articles

Argyris, N., 'The EEC Rules of Competition and the Air Transport Sector' (1989) 26 CMLRev 5-32

Balfour, J., 'Freedom to provide Air Transport Services in the EEC' (1989) ELRev 30-46

— 'Air Transport – a Community success story?' (1994) 31 CMLRev 1025-53

Bellis, J. E., E. Vermulst, and P. Musquar, 'New EEC Regulation on Unfair Pricing Practices in Maritime Transport: a forerunner of the extension of unfair trade concepts to services?' (1988) WTL 47

Blonk, W., 'Applying rules of competition to transport by rail, road and inland waterway (Regulation 1017/68)' (1969) 6 CMLRev 451-65

Brandt, E. and P. Schafer, 'Trans-Alpine Traffic: Towards Sustainable Mobility' (1996) CMLRev 931-72

Bredimas, A., 'The Common Shipping Policy of the EEC' (1981) 18 CMLRev 9

Button, K. and D. Swann, 'European Community Airlines – Deregulation and its Problems' (1989) Journal of Common Market Studies 259-82

Churchill, R. 'European Community Law and the Nationality of Ships and Crew in European transport Law' (1991) Journal of Law and Economics 591-617

Clinton Davies, S. 'Transport Policy and the 1990s' 3/88 European Affairs 39-45

Close, G. 'The development of transport policy in the sea and air sectors' (1980) ELRev 188

— 'External Relations in the Air Transport sector: Air Transport Policy or the Common Commercial Policy?' (1990) CMLRev 106-27

Collinson, D. S., 'Economic regulation of transport under the Common Transport Policy' (1972) 24 Stanford LRev 221-346

Dagtoglou, P. D., 'Air transport and the European Community' (1981) ELRev 335-55

Fennel, P. 'The transport policy case' (1985) ELRev 264-76

Goh, J., 'External Relations in Community Air Transport: a Policy Analysis' (1996) European Public Law 453-76

Greaves, R., 'Judicial Review of Commisison Decisions on State Aids to Airlines', ch. 39 in *Liber Amicorum for Gordon Slynn* (2000)

Johnson, M. A., 'Removing Barriers to Market Entry in the Air Transport Industry: the Application of EC Competition Rules' (1993) Legal Issues of European Integration 1-34

Kark, A. 'Prospects for a Liberalisation of the European Air Transport Industry: A Study of Commercial Air Transport Policy for the European Community' (1989) ECLR 377-406

Lewis, X., 'Vers le marche unique des transports' (1991) Revue du Marche Unique 49-84

Riphagen, W., 'The Transport Legislation of the European Communities, its Relationship to International Treaties and its Effect in Member States' (1966) 3 CMLRev 291-325

Robert, J., 'Doubts on a Common Transport Policy' (1968) 5 CMLRev 193-207

Stabenow, W., 'The Common Market for Transport in the European Economic Community' (1964) 1 CMLRev 391-405

Strivens, R. and E. Weightman, 'The Air Transport Sector and the EEC Competition Rules in the Light of the *Ahmed Saeed* Case' (1989) ECLRev 557-67

Trinion, J., 'Community Transport Law: the current position' (1975) ELRev 77-82

Van Houtte, B., 'Relevant Markets in Air Transport' (1990) 27 CMLRev 521-46

Weinreb, A., 'The special aspects of transport and the Treaty of Rome' (1974) 19 Law Society Gazette 462-63

Zekos, G., 'The Implementation of EU Competition Policy and its Rules in Air and Maritime Transport' (1998) ECLRev 430-42

FURTHER READING

General

Bredima-Savopoulou, A. and J. Tzoanos, (1990) *The Common Shipping Policy of the EC* (North-Holland, Amsterdam)

Erdmenger, J., (1983) *The European Community Transport Policy: Towards a CTP* (Gower, London)

Power, V., (1992) *EC Shipping Law* (Lloyd's, London)

Competition

Argyris, N., 'The EEC Rules of Competition and the Air Transport Sector' (1989) CMLRev 5-32

Bellis, J. E., E. Vermulst and P. Musquar, 'New EEC Regulation on Unfair Pricing Practices in Maritime Transport: a forerunner of the extension of unfair trade concepts to services?' (1988) WTL 47

Blonk, W., 'Applying rules of competition to transport by rail, road and inland waterway (Regulation 1017/68)' (1969) 6 CMLRev 451-65

Craig, P. and G. de Burca, *EU Law: Text, Cases and Materials* (2nd ed., 1998, OUP, Oxford), chs 20-23.

Goh, J., *European Air Transport Law and Competition* (1997, Wiley, Chichester)

Goyder, D. G., *EEC Competition Law* (2nd ed., 1993, OUP, Oxford)

Greaves, R., 'Judicial Review of Commission Decisions on State Aids to Airlines', ch. 39 in *Liber Amicorum for Gordon Slynn* (2000)

Korah, V., *EC Competition Law and Practice* (1994, Sweet & Maxwell, London)

Strivens, R. and E. Weightman, 'The Air Transport Sector and the EEC Competition Rules in the Light of the *Ahmed Saeed* Case' (1989) ECLRev 557-67

Whish, R., *Competition Law* (3rd ed., 1993, Butterworths, London)

Zekos, G., 'The Implementation of EU Competition Policy and its Rules in Air and Maritime Transport' (1998) ECLRev 430-42

INDEX